D1439513

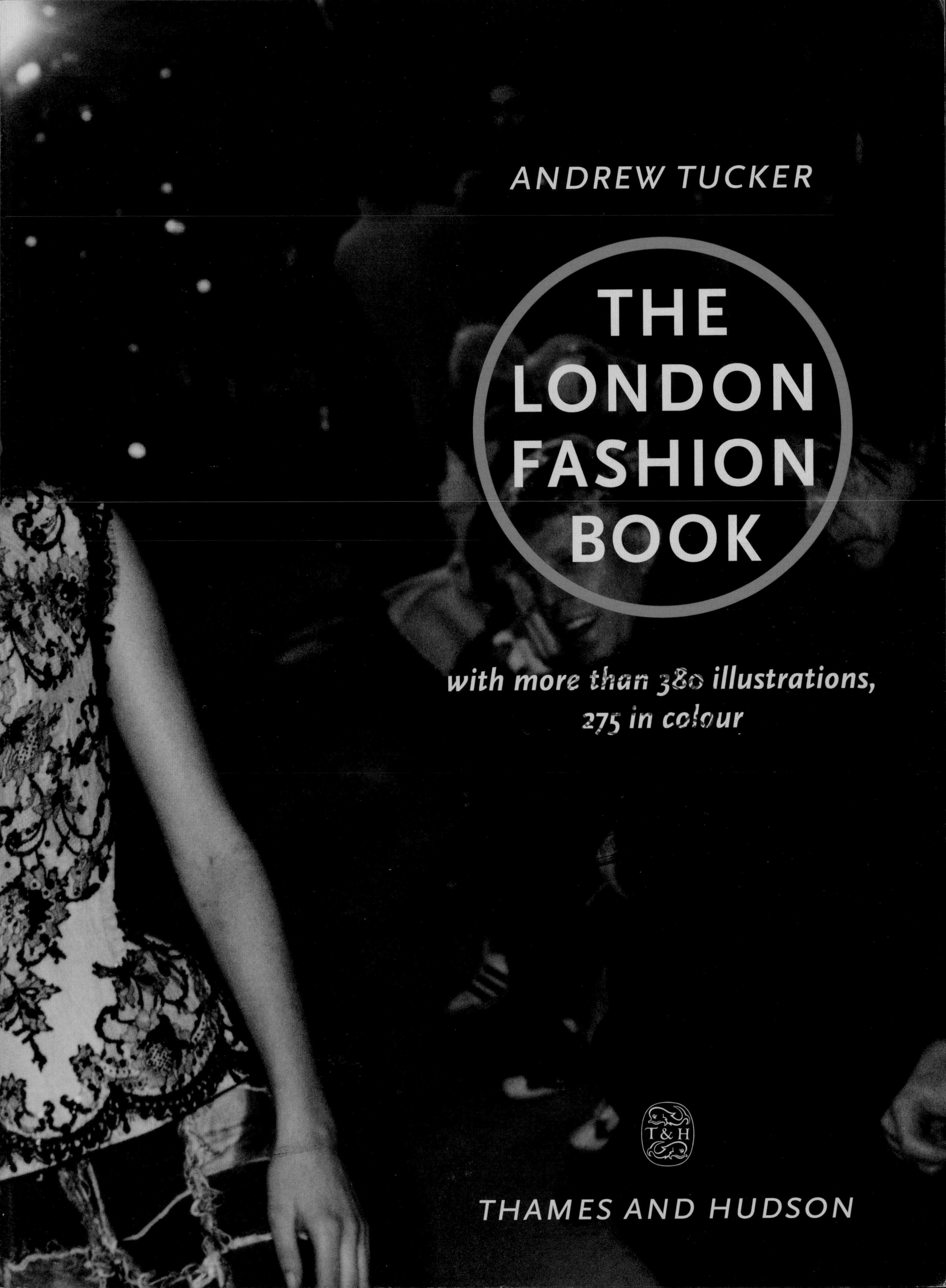

ANDREW TUCKER

# THE LONDON FASHION BOOK

with more than 380 illustrations,
275 in colour

THAMES AND HUDSON

*HALF-TITLE: John Galliano,
Autumn/Winter 1997–98.*
Photo Anne Deniau, 1997.

*TITLE SPREAD: Alexander
McQueen, Autumn/Winter
1996–97, 'Dante' collection.*
Photo Mark C. O'Flaherty.

*CONTENTS PAGES:*
Photo Wanda Roslini.

*FOLLOWING PAGES:*
Photo Dafydd Jones.

© 1998 Thames and Hudson Ltd,
London

British Library Cataloguing-in-
Publication Data
A catalogue record for this book is
available from the British Library

ISBN 0 – 500 – 28071 – 1

Printed in Hong Kong by
H&Y Printing Ltd

DEDICATED TO
LW, CL, CT & JN

# CONTENTS

BEFORE
THE
SHOW

**above, clockwise from top left:** Odile Gilbert, hair artist, at work at the Galliano for Givenchy Haute Couture A/W 1996–97 collection in July 1996 at the Stade Français, Paris. Photo Anne Deniau, 1996 • • • Stella Tennant at Philip Treacy, October 1993. Photo Niall McInerney • • • Kate Moss at Chloé, October 1997. Photo Jonathan West • • • Oguri S/S 1998 collection, shown at the Brompton Oratory, 25 September 1997. Photo Adrian Wilson • • • • Ben de Lisi, S/S 1998 collection. Photo Tim Griffiths • • • • Hair artist Nicolas Jurnjack creating Stella Tennant's hairstyle at the McQueen for Givenchy Haute Couture collection for A/W 1997–98 at the Faculté de Médecine, Paris. Photo Anne Deniau, 1997 • • • Galliano 'Suzy Sphinx' collection for A/W 1997–98 at the Musée des Monuments Français, Paris, March 1997. Photo Anne Deniau, 1997

**this page, clockwise from top left:** Clements Ribeiro show at Imperial College, London, 27 September 1997. Photo Dafydd Jones • • • • • • • Model Carla Bruni reflected in the mirror at the McQueen for Givenchy Prêt-à-porter show for A/W 1997–98. Photo Anne Deniau, 1997 • • • • • At Fabio Piras, S/S May 1998. Photo Tim Griffiths • • • Esther Canadas being made up for the McQueen for Givenchy S/S 1998 Prêt-à-porter collection in October 1997 at the Stade Français, Paris. Photo Anne Deniau, 1997 • • • At the McQueen for Givenchy S/S 1998 Prêt-à-porter collection. Photo Jonathan West • • • • • • • • Chrystelle and Naomi at the McQueen for Givenchy A/W 1997–98 Prêt-à-porter collection. Photo Anne Deniau, 1997 • • • • • • • • • • • • • • • • • • • • • • • • • • • • • • • • • • • • • • • • • • • • • • • • •

IT'S THE NIGHT BEFORE THE SHOW, AND THE WORKROOM TEAM HAS ADJOURNED FOR A WELL-EARNED RESPITE FROM THE CHAOS OF THE PREVIOUS WEEK. THE BALE OF LACE HAS FINALLY ARRIVED FROM SWITZERLAND, THE FITTINGS HAVE BEEN COMPLETED, AND THE ONLY PROBLEMS STILL TO BE IRONED OUT ARE THE CREASES ON A SHOULDERPAD. AT THE VENUE ITSELF, DRAPERIES ARE ERECTED, GILT CHAIRS ASCRIBED AND HANDWRITTEN PLACE CARDS DAINTILY POSITIONED ON EACH PADDED VELVET SEAT. THE SILENCE IS EERIE. IN LESS THAN TWELVE HOURS THE ROOM WILL REVERBERATE WITH CAMERA SHUTTERS, MOBILE PHONES AND UNPLACEABLE ACCENTS. TONIGHT IT IS INHABITED ONLY BY GHOSTS • • • • • • • • • • • • • • • • • • • • • • • • • • • • • • • • • • • • • • • • • • • • • • • • • • • • • • • • • • • • • • •

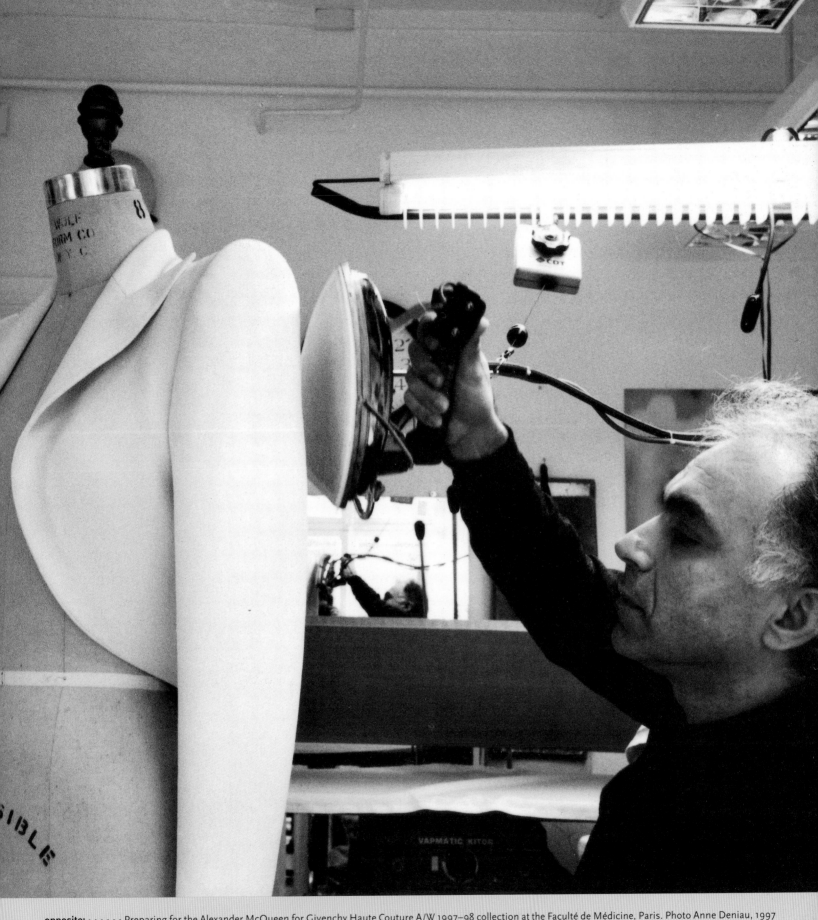

*BACKSTAGE AT A SHOW IS LIKE WATCHING A SOCCER TEAM PREPARE TO PASS THE MODEL, LIKE A FOOTBALL, FROM THE DEPTHS OF THE FIELD TO THE GOAL AT THE MOUTH OF THE CATWALK. SHE IS PRIMPED, PREENED AND DRESSED IN READINESS. SUDDENLY THE WHISTLE BLOWS – AND THE DESIGNER PREPARES TO STRIKE* **this page, clockwise from top left:** Hair artist Nicolas Jurnjack with Naomi Campbell before the Alexander McQueen for Givenchy Haute Couture collection for S/S 1997 at the Ecole des Beaux-Arts, Paris. Photo Anne Deniau, 1997 • • • • • • • • At Stella McCartney's S/S 1997 collection, held in McCartney's studio in Notting Hill Gate. Photo Mary McCartney • • • Honor Fraser at the Clements Ribeiro S/S 1997 collection. Photo Tim Griffiths • • • • • • • • • • • • • • • • • At the Ghost collection for S/S 1998. Photo Tim Griffiths

**this page, clockwise from top left:** A bathroom doubles as a changing room at Stella McCartney's S/S 1997 collection. Photo Mary McCartney • • • • • • • • At Joe Casely-Hayford's show at the Institute of Directors, London 1997. Photo Dafydd Jones • • • • • • • Rifat Ozbek A/W 1996–97. Photo Gavin Bond • • • • • • • • Manolo Blahnik shoes for Antonio Berardi's S/S 1998 collection; behind are Polaroids showing the running order of the show. Photo Gavin Bond • • • • • • • • Eva Herzigova taking a nap at a Vivienne Westwood collection. Photo Gavin Bond • • • • • • • • Jodie Kidd at Ben de Lisi's collection for A/W 1997–98. Photo Tim Griffiths • • • • • • • • • • • • • • • • • • • • • • • • • • • • • • • • • • • • • • • • • • • • • • • • • • • • • • • • • • • • • • • • • • • • • • •

IT'S A COOL EVENING IN LATE SEPTEMBER, AND THE GREEN HARRODS BUS DISGORGES TIRED JOURNALISTS LIKE A TROOP CARRIER IN A WAR ZONE. IT'S THE ALEXANDER MCQUEEN SHOW, AND IT'S RUNNING LATE. THE CROWD IS TEN DEEP AND ANGRY. NOBODY, BUT NOBODY, IS GETTING IN WITHOUT A TICKET — AND YET THOSE CLUTCHING THE TREASURED ENTRY CARD ARE BLOCKED BY GROUPIES, STUDENTS AND CURIOUS PASSERS-BY. OVERTURES OF FRIENDSHIP, PROFFERED CREDENTIALS AND NOISY INDIGNATION FALL ON DEAF EARS. SOME PLEAD WITH THE SECURITY GUARD; OTHERS PUSH SLOWLY FORWARD. BACKSTAGE A GENERATOR CRANKS UP, AND A BEAM OF LIGHT ILLUMINATES THE CROWD. THE TITLE OF THE SHOW IS 'IT'S A JUNGLE OUT THERE', WHICH PROVES TO BE THE UNDERSTATEMENT OF LONDON FASHION WEEK. DURING THE

ENSUING HYSTERIA THE BARRIER IS SMASHED AND THE CROWD SURGES FORWARD. BODIES ARE CRUSHED, TRAMPLED AND PUSHED ASIDE IN A PANIC TO SEE THE FIRST

OUTFIT. WHEN YOU'RE THIS OBSESSED, NOTHING MATTERS BUT TAKING PART IN THE MOMENT. SO WHAT IF IT MEANS GETTING A BROKEN ANKLE? – THAT'S FASHION • • • • •

**main picture:** Part of the crowd trying to gain admittance to the Alexander McQueen show at Borough Market, London SE1, on 27 February 1997. Photo Dafydd Jones • • • •

• • • • • • • • • • • • • • • • • • • • • • • • **above:** The art director, illustrator and photographer Michael Roberts (centre), waiting for the Owen Gaster show to begin on 24

February 1997 at the Natural History Museum, London. Photo Dafydd Jones • • • • • • • • • • • • • • • • • • • • • • • • • • • • • • • • • • • • • • • • • • • • • • •

DURING LONDON'S FIRST GOLDEN age of fashion, in the 1960s and 1970s, very few of the current crop of designers who are included here would have been more than schoolchildren, while those who were luminaries at that time are now more suited to retrospectives than to an analysis of the contemporary. And yet, without the ground-breaking work of the designers of the past forty years – Norman Hartnell, Ossie Clark, Mary Quant, Barbara Hulanicki, Thea Porter, Body Map, Richmond Cornejo, John Flett, Bill Gibb and others, British fashion would not have the reputation for innovative and exciting design that it currently enjoys.

Today, London is the most scrutinized fashion capital in the world. It has produced talents such as John Galliano and Alexander McQueen, now officially in residence at the houses of Dior and Givenchy. London Fashion Week (once home to a surfeit of tired ballgowns) has been transformed from a fashion pit stop to an essential rendezvous for the international press and buying communities. What are the magic ingredients that have made London worthy of such enormous hype and attention, and why does it generate such prodigious talent when other fashion capitals are deemed to be at so low an ebb?

The answer is twofold: the British design education system, which provides a nursery of ideas, and our capital city itself – the most sprawling, multifaceted metropolis in the world, which has benefited artistically from the mixture of nationalities and cultures that make up its population. Coupled together, these two disparate elements have produced designers of the calibre of Westwood, McQueen, Treacy and Galliano, not to mention a host of new creative talents who are snapping at their heels each season.

*The London Fashion Book* is a comprehensive guide to the personalities and places that typify British fashion at the end of the millennium. It is meant neither as a reference book nor as a textbook (though it can serve as either), but rather as a documentary of a period when British style stood at the vanguard of contemporary culture. It should be viewed as a time capsule – a celebration of fashion's moment in the sun.

Since fashion is more linked to the process of time and change than any other artistic medium, London's moment may not last for ever. The press may grow tired of the 'edgy' looks popularized by our newest generation of talent, and move on. But British fashion would continue to have an effect on the hearts and minds of the fashion fraternity. For were Milan, Paris or New York to become the next 'Big Thing', the engines of design houses worldwide would still be fuelled by British graduates quietly creating masterpieces behind the scenes.

*The London Fashion Book* aims to give the reader an insight into both the work and the characters of our most exciting designers, and to explore the milieu in which they operate as well as the world of muses, stylists, art directors, photographers and illustrators who sustain them. What would Chloé's Stella McCartney do without the markets of Portobello Road, where she rummages for antique trims with which to embellish her simple slip dresses? Where would Tomasz Starzewski be without his coterie of Knightsbridge ladies-who-lunch? To whom would Alexander McQueen boast of his East End roots and (supposed) descent from a victim of Jack the Ripper? They, and many others, are products of their environment – and that environment is London.

The seven fashionable areas of London on which we have focused in this book are as varied as the designers themselves and show what important roles the city plays – with its shops, markets, restaurants, bars and nightclubs – in the theatre of London fashion.

The designers have been broadly categorized into type, ranging from the flamboyant in Haute Hippie to the classicists who make up the Thoroughbreds. Despite a reticence to pigeonhole any of them, we have employed these categories to give structure to the book and to facilitate the reader's progress through it. The groupings are necessarily loose – some designers fit as well into one as another – but they are there to express the enormous diversity of style that constitutes British fashion today. As to the question: what is British?, the designers whose work is shown here include not only those who have been born and bred within the vicinity of the M25 Motorway, but those who, although their origins lie abroad, remain intrinsically associated with the capital.

Beautiful and fickle, fashion will go on changing its boundaries without warning. But no matter what becomes of the London scene, *The London Fashion Book* will serve as a reminder of how it is, how it was, and how it could be again in the future.

OPPOSITE: *Illustration by Demetrios Psillos.*

OVERLEAF: *London Fashion Map by Jason Brooks.*

192

Lisboa

Griffin

Beach Blanket Babylon

Portobello Road

Ladbroke Grove

Pembridge Road

Notting Hill

Bayswater
the Tempel

Edgware Road

St Christopher's Place
whistles

Portland Place

Notting Hill Gate

Bayswater Rd

Oxford Street

Liberty

Kensington Church St

Kensington
Gardens

Park Lane

Mayfair

South Molton St.

Vogue House

VOGUE

Regent Street

BAR

Holland
Park

Hyde
Park

Savile
Row

Kensington High Street

Knightsbridge

Hyde Park
Corner

Piccadilly

Kensington

Gloucester Road

London Fashion week

Royal College
of Art

V&A

Brompton Road

Harrods

Beauchamp Place

Sloane Street

Harvey Nichols

Grosvenor Place

Green
Park

Pall M

the
St J

Buckingham
Palace

Cromwell Road

Old Brompton Road

Fulham Road

Voyage

Peter Jones

Sloane Square

Belgravia

Eaton Square

Victoria

Westm

the
Tate

Vauxhall Bridge Road

TAXI

Fulham

King's Road

World's End

Chelsea

Pimlico

PASSPORT

Chelsea Bridge Road

Grosvenor Road

Chelsea Bridge

River

WEST
END

Photo Dafydd Jones.

LONDON'S 'ARTY PARTY' SET EXISTS ON A DIET OF VODKA, CHAMPAGNE AND CANAPÉS. ENTRY TO THIS SELECT GROUP REQUIRES NOTHING MORE THAN CELEBRITY, GLAMOUR OR A HEFTY BANK BALANCE. **this page, clockwise from top left:** Naomi Campbell, October 1997. Photo Jonathan West • • • • • • • Mick Jagger and Liam Gallagher at the *Vanity Fair* 'Swinging London' dinner at the River Café, London, 20 November 1996. Photo Dafydd Jones • • • • • • Damien Hirst, Louise Wilson, Maia Morgan (Hirst's wife) and Jane Wilson at the Serpentine Gallery fundraiser on 28 June 1995. Photo Dafydd Jones • • • • • • • • Models relaxing in Stella McCartney's studio. Photo Mary McCartney • • • • • • • • Tracey Emin at the 'Sensation' exhibition, Royal Academy of Art, September 1997. Photo James Peltekian • • • • • • • • Johnnie Shand Kydd at the Turner Prize

awards ceremony, Tate Gallery, 28 November 1996. Photo Dafydd Jones • • • • • • • • • • • • • **this page, top:** Model Georgina Cooper relaxes after a show, October 1997. Photo Jonathan West • • • • • • • • **centre strip, left to right:** Boy George (photo Mark C. O'Flaherty); Sara Stockbridge (photo Dafydd Jones); Jerry Hall (photo Dafydd Jones); Tamara Beckwith (photo Mark C. O'Flaherty); Lorenzo Agius (photo Dafydd Jones); Zandra Rhodes (photo Mark C. O'Flaherty); Jarvis Cocker (photo James Peltekian); Yasmin le Bon (photo Mark C. O'Flaherty); Steve Shaw and Lili Maltese (photo Dafydd Jones) • • • • • • • • • • • • • • **bottom right:** Michael Roberts talks to Isabella Blow at the *Vanity Fair* 'Swinging London' dinner at the River Café, London, on 20 November 1996. Photo Dafydd Jones • • • • • **bottom left:** The party's over. Photo Jonathan West

IN AMONG THE BARE-CHESTED RAVERS IN LONDON'S CLUBLAND IS A STYLE. IT'S IMPOSSIBLE TO DEFINE AND CONSTANTLY CHANGING, YET IT REFLECTS FASHION FROM THE STREET AND PROVIDES INSPIRATION FOR DESIGNERS WHO CONSTANTLY PLUNDER THE WEALTH OF IDEAS IT ORIGINATES. IF YOU LOOK CLOSELY YOU MAY SEE JEAN-PAUL GAULTIER FURIOUSLY SKETCHING IN A CORNER, OR, MAKING THEIR WAY ACROSS THE DANCE FLOOR, A JAPANESE TV CREW REPORTING ON LONDON STREET STYLE • • • • • • • • THE STYLE THAT EVOLVES IN LONDON CLUBS IS NOT FOUND ABROAD. BRITISH CLUBBERS KNOW HOW TO PUT A LOOK TOGETHER, HOW TO MIX DESIGNER CLOTHES WITH SECOND-HAND GEAR OR COMBINE CHAINSTORE ITEMS WITH ARMY SURPLUS. WHAT ALSO MAKES LONDON'S CLUBLAND UNIQUE IS ITS EVER-CHANGING FACE AND ITS DIVERSE

VENUES, CATERING TO EVERY POSSIBLE TASTE. THERE ARE SO MANY CLUBS TODAY THAT YOU COULD VISIT A NEW ONE EVERY NIGHT FOR A YEAR. EACH HAS ITS OWN STYLE AND DEVOTEES, FROM DRAG KINGS (GAY WOMEN EMULATING MEN) TO ESSEX BOYS ON A SATURDAY NIGHT OUT • • • • • • • • • • • • • • • • • • • • • • • • • •

**opposite top left:** Party atmosphere at the Katharine Hamnett S/S 1998 collection. Photo Dee Jay • • • • • • • • • • • • • • • • • • • • • • • • • • • • • • • •

**opposite centre left:** Keeping out the riff-raff. Photo Dafydd Jones • • • • • • • • • • • • • • **remaining pictures:** Pushca at the Ministry of Sound. Photos Richard Fawcett

• • • • • • • • • • • • • • • • • • • • • • • • • • • • • • • • • • • • • •

IT'S ALMOST CLOSING TIME, AND ONLY THE DRUNKEST REVELLER WOULD DANCE TO THE SMOOCHIES THAT THE DJ SPINS IN AN EFFORT TO CLEAR THE DANCEFLOOR.

TONIGHT WAS GOOD — YOU DANCED TO YOUR FAVOURITE TUNES, TOUCHED BASE WITH YOUR MATES, AND AVOIDED SPENDING FAR TOO MUCH MONEY ON EXORBITANTLY

PRICED ALCOHOL AT THE BAR. BUT IT'S BEEN A LONG NIGHT. PAVEMENTS ARE LITTERED WITH BRIGHT FLYERS, EACH ONE TRYING TO SURPASS THE OTHER IN COLOURFUL

PRINT AND LANGUAGE. SCATTERED ALONG REGENT STREET, CLUBBERS HUDDLE TOGETHER — THE STROBELIGHTS AND VELVET BANQUETTES OF THEIR FAVOURED HOT-SPOT

REPLACED BY CONDENSATION AND CRAMPED NIGHT-BUS SEATS. ALL ARE GOING HOME TO STREETS OF QUIET HOUSES, BEYOND THE PLEASURE PALACES OF THE WEST END,

FOR TEA, TOAST AND KITCHEN CONVERSATIONS. EVERY PASSING TAXI IS FULL, AND, AS YOU LOOK AROUND, FELLOW PARTY-GOERS ARE QUEUEING FOR POUND-A-SLICE PIZZA AND DUBIOUS KEBABS THAT WILL SOAK UP ALCOHOL BUT BE REGRETTED IN THE MORNING. IT'S ALL PART OF A RITUAL — THE PLEASURE OF A NIGHT OUT IN LONDON IS INVARIABLY COMBINED WITH A HANGOVER AND INDIGESTION. BUT, LIKE ANY OTHER SENSATION-SEEKER, YOU'LL BE BACK FOR MORE NEXT SATURDAY NIGHT — AND THE SATURDAY AFTER THAT • • • • • • • **opposite:** West End clubbers and party-goers at Freedom Café Bar, Bar Italia and Soho Brasserie. Photos Tim Griffiths, 1997 • • • • • • • • •

**above:** Miles in Soho, in double-layered sleeveless T-shirt by Copperwheat Blundell. Photo Rick Guest, 1997 • • • • • • • • • • • • • • • • • • • • • • • •

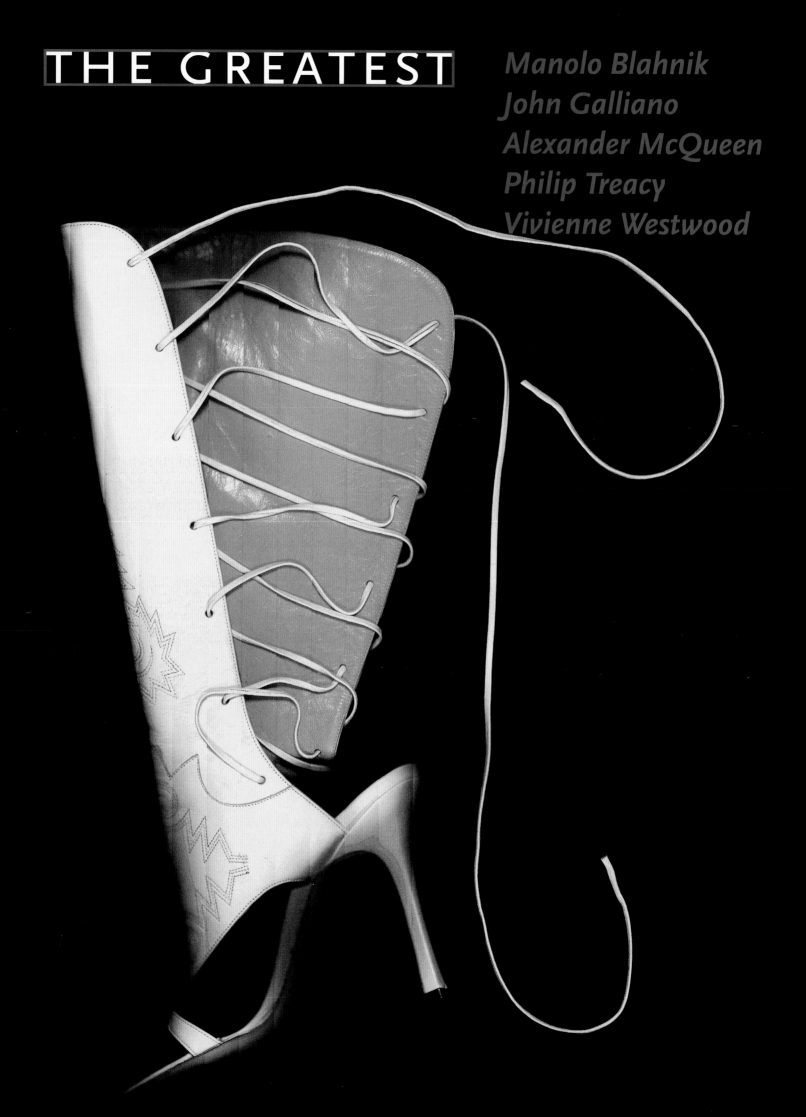

# THE GREATEST

*Manolo Blahnik*

*John Galliano*

*Alexander McQueen*

*Philip Treacy*

*Vivienne Westwood*

# VIVIENNE WESTWOOD

Vivienne Westwood is the UK's most maverick
designer, included by publishing guru John Fairchild
of *Womenswear Daily* in his list of the six most creative
minds in fashion. Though the audience tittered at
her designs on primetime television, she has had a
greater influence on our dressing habits than we could
ever imagine.

Since the 1970s, when the first bondage trousers
struggled out of her World's End boutique, she has
left an indelible mark on British fashion. From pirates
in asymmetrical T-shirts in 1981 through to shapes
derived from 16th-century costume in her 'Five
Centuries' collection for Autumn/Winter 1997–98,
she has challenged our preconceptions about what
fashion might be. She has brought back the platform
shoe, invented the mini-crini, padded busts and
derrières, and made tartan trendy.

Westwood claims that she has no interest in or
knowledge of what other designers are doing, and she
works from an almost self-imposed creative insularity,
one that is currently engaged in exploring and
reinventing historical dress in a modern way. 'In my
collection "Vive la Cocotte", the false bottoms, padded
busts and high heels were taken from an historical
concept, and then combined to form a brand-new
silhouette,' she says. And, despite an almost formulaic
approach to show production (heady classical music,
historically inspired hair and make-up and a venue
where velvet drapery seems never to be absent), the
clothes themselves are indeed surprisingly modern
and easily understood when seen in the showroom.
Today's Westwood is a far cry from the punk priestess
who offered salvation from the disco-obsessed fashions
of the late 1970s. She is cultured and sedate, and exudes
a matronly air of eccentricity that owes more to the
twinset and pearls brigade than to Home Counties
anarchists. 'With the whole punk thing, I realized that
by attacking the establishment I'd become a victim; the
only true way to make a difference is through ideas, not

ABOVE: One of the many faces of
Vivienne Westwood – the elegant
but 'distressed' punk priestess,
photographed on a park bench
in London, wearing a pair of her
super-elevated courts.
Photo Juergen Teller, for
French Vogue, 1995.

<< PRECEDING PAGES
*Left: Manolo Blahnik for Clements
Ribeiro, Spring/Summer 1998.
Photo Katerina Jebb.*

*Right: Dress by Alexander
McQueen; jewelry by Sarah
Harmanee for Alexander
McQueen, Autumn/Winter
1997–98.
Photo Sean Ellis.*

'The innovators challenge orthodoxy. Chanel's clothes physically liberated woman. Saint Laurent's gave her a sense of power. Westwood's provide an ironic mask with which she can project many personae and behind which she can hide her vulnerabilities and even her ordinariness' JANE MULVAGH, FASHION HISTORIAN

rebellion,' she says. And yet, if you look closely, her designs are still mildly subversive. A traditional Harris tweed jacket has exaggerated proportions or armour-like inferences; a cabbage rose chintz is printed on latex, a twinset appears in a menswear collection. Add to that all the ideas which the high street has taken and diluted into more saleable forms and you begin to see her massive influence.

In 1971 Vivienne Westwood was running up teddy-boy and fifties-inspired clothes on a sewing machine in the back of Let It Rock, the shop she ran with Malcolm McLaren in World's End, on the King's Road, Chelsea. Today she heads a hugely successful company, one which includes couture, ready-to-wear, menswear, casual wear and accessories. She has spearheaded British design throughout Europe, and her greatest achievement is that she has managed to do so without selling her soul.

LEFT: Vivienne Westwood, outside the Victoria and Albert Museum in the late 1980s, wearing the fig-leaf tights which caused a furore when she appeared in them on primetime television.
Photo Solo Syndication Ltd.

ABOVE: Red portrait jacket, cut and slash leather corset, and skirt with codpiece. From the 'Dressing Up' collection of Autumn/Winter 1991–92.
Photo Trevor Sears, courtesy Vivienne Westwood.

OPPOSITE: Portrait of Anna Malni, actress and photographer, wearing a Westwood design. Hair and make-up by Darren Evans.
Photo Jonathan Root, 1995.

*LEFT: 'Vive la Bagatelle', Gold Label Spring/Summer 1997 collection, held at the Louvre, Paris, in October 1996. 'It's about flirting . . . a trifle, a nothing, a ribbon; a bow tied prettily and easily undone.'*
Photo Gavin Bond.

*THIS PAGE: 'To Rosie', Red Label Autumn/Winter 1997–98 collection, held at the Dorchester Hotel, London, in September 1997.*
Photos Gavin Bond.

# ALEXANDER McQUEEN

'The irreverent Alexander McQueen has the best sense of proportion (visually and emotionally) of any fashion designer today'

RICHARD MARTIN, CURATOR,

THE COSTUME INSTITUTE, THE METROPOLITAN MUSEUM OF ART

Alexander McQueen is bored with the clichés used about him in the press ('East End Boy Made Good', 'Savile Row Apprentice', etc.) and he's had enough of all the newspaper stories that focus on the drama of events surrounding his clothes rather than the clothes themselves.

But can he really complain? After all, shock tactics and hell-raising show productions have made him, at an extremely early age, an international figure on the designer circuit.

Perhaps what he really objects to is that all the fuss obscures the fact that he is an enormously talented designer. From making a new erogenous zone of the buttock – with his cleavage-revealing bumster trousers – to creating highly commercial pieces that look great on real women, McQueen has made a notable contribution to the fashion industry.

But though he has already produced more memorable garments than many designers will manage in a lifetime, it was not until 1996 that McQueen was able to produce his first collection commercially. His ready-to-wear business is growing every season, a fact which, he says, a lot of people don't realize because they are 'more interested in the show production than in the clothes'. Nowadays his fans range from celebrities, to older women who buy the structured brocade jackets, to regular punters looking for a slashed T-shirt with a zip front, or an imperial dragon devoréd onto a column of black velvet.

Needless to say, despite the desirable pieces that turn up every season, it is the statement-making clothes that give McQueen his reputation for being dangerous: the jeweled manacles that held a model like an exotic slave in his Spring/Summer 1997 collection, 'Bellmer La Poupée' and the dishevelled models in tattered lace in his Highland Rape collection of 1995–96.

McQueen may indeed have exhibitionist tendencies. The shows are dramatic feats in themselves: models have been known to wade through water, strut past the burning shells of wrecked cars or bring disquiet to the assembled audience by wearing opaque contact lenses or prosthetic horns glued to their heads. Part of McQueen's attraction lies in the fact that his shows fall in a territory between fantasy and reality. There are enough elements of real clothing to qualify the show as a fashion collection, but there is always the added frisson of the strange and the forbidden.

BELOW: Greta Cavazzoni (with Karen Elson at top of stairs) on the way to the catwalk at the Givenchy Haute Couture collection for Autumn/Winter 1997–98.

RIGHT, TOP: The venue of the Givenchy Haute Couture collection for Autumn/Winter 1997–98.

THIS PAGE, REMAINING PICTURES: Ateliers Givenchy, for Haute Couture Spring/Summer 1997.

OPPOSITE LEFT, TOP TO BOTTOM: Givenchy Prêt-à-porter Autumn/ Winter 1997–98 at the Parc Georges Brassens, Paris.

OPPOSITE BOTTOM RIGHT-HAND CORNER: Kate Moss at the Givenchy Prêt-à-porter Spring/ Summer 1998 collection at the Stade Français, Paris.

REMAINING PICTURES: Givenchy Haute Couture collection Autumn/Winter 1997–98 at the Faculté de Médecine, Paris. All photos Anne Deniau, 1997.

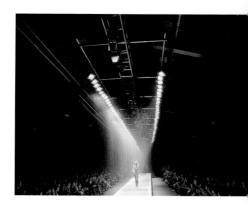

McQueen's show for Spring/Summer 1998 – one of the most dramatic fashion shows ever staged – was art-directed by Simon Costin.

Costin describes the evolution of the staging as follows: 'I showed McQueen a section from the film *2001*, where the astronauts first encounter the monolith in the crater on the moon. I wanted people to feel that they were entering an unearthly, almost religious space where an enormous amount of energy was contained, but only just. It had to feel potentially dangerous. In real terms this was actually the case as the combination of hundreds of live fluorescent tubes and gallons of water supported by a perspex structure that weighed over forty tons could have been very dangerous. I started by making a scale model that was shown to the plastic fabricators. There were twelve identical tanks made from 20mm-thick perspex standing on a scaffolding base. The tanks were lit from beneath by over a thousand individual fluorescent tubes. Alexander decided he wanted the models in the second half to get wet, so we installed a rain machine. The stylist Katy England had the unenviable job of walking along underneath it while we adjusted the degree of water that fell.

In the end I suggested that we introduce a negative visual element – negative in terms of being a reversal of what we already had as far as the lighting was concerned. I had read quite broadly on the subject of alchemy and my early notes for the show included copies of some drawings by the 17th-century alchemist Robert Fludd. Fludd was greatly influenced by John Dee, Elizabeth I's court physician and alchemist.

Since the collection turned from mainly dark colours in the first half to white in the second, I suggested that we pump black ink into the tanks during a three-minute interval. At this point there were no models on the catwalk and the whole structure became like an installation in its own right as the tanks slowly filled with billowing clouds of black which obscured the light below, fulfilling the alchemical saying: 'As above so below.' This was accompanied by the sound of dripping water and the ominous *Jaws* theme. Finally, to a dramatic drum roll, a model appeared as the lights turned to gold and a cascade of water fell from the rig above. The rain was heated from a tank backstage and lasted until the show had finished.'

# JOHN GALLIANO

If Hollywood were to make a movie of John Galliano's life and career, it would have all the elements of a blockbuster: rags to riches, tortured genius and high glamour, not to mention some ingredients that might earn it an 18 certificate. In true celebrity style, he is the darling of the contemporary fashion press, yet his creativity is born not out of a love of the modern, but of the antique.

Galliano is a fantasist whose talent derives from an obsession with history that encompasses every epoch in the quest to reinvent concepts of historical costume for a modern-day audience. 'I'm a romantic at heart,' he says, 'and I hope that this can be felt in my clothes. Fashion is like music to me, in that it's about feeling. I want people to be moved by my clothes in the same way that they would be moved by music. Ultimately, I see myself as an accomplice to women who enjoy dressing up and celebrating their own femininity.'

He has been extremely successful in achieving this dream. For though muses like Kiki de Montparnasse may have little relevance for today's audience, Galliano has made the forgotten skills employed by their dressmakers once again common currency. Because of him, bias cutting is now *de rigueur*. His former assistants (many now designing their own collections) cannot shake off his influences; the intensely romantic silhouette, the complexity of the cut and, of course, the painstaking attention to historical detail.

Galliano's June 1984 degree collection was such a smash hit that the London boutique Browns bought it in its entirety, launching a successful career in the lucrative days of the mid-eighties. Though backers came and went, Galliano gained a cult following and eventually decamped to Paris. Latterly Givenchy and subsequently Dior employed him to design both ready-to-wear and couture collections. 'I've probably had three definitive moments in my career to date,' he says, 'The first was when Mrs Burstein of Browns bought my final-year collection and placed it in the window. The second was my Autumn/Winter 1994–95 collection. Three weeks before the shows, when it looked as if I might not be able to put a collection together because I had no financial partner, I found the money to make my collection through the help of Anna Wintour and André Leon Talley of American *Vogue*. I did only seventeen outfits, all in black except two, since black fabric was the easiest to get hold of at such short notice. Sao Schlumberger lent me her *maison particulière*, which gave the show a salon feeling. The collection itself was

OPPOSITE: *John Galliano for Dior Couture: dress in satin double face with embroideries and appliqué, Spring/Summer 1997.* Photo Sean Ellis.

ABOVE: *John Galliano, Autumn/Winter 1997–98.* Photo Anne Deniau, 1997.

'A brilliant subjective historicist from the outset, Galliano has increasingly assimilated all his historical paradigms. Thus, Galliano's *dix-huitième* today embraces Vionnet and exoticisms in fantastic pastiche'

RICHARD MARTIN, CURATOR, THE COSTUME INSTITUTE, THE METROPOLITAN MUSEUM OF ART

OPPOSITE: *Dior Couture,*
*Spring/Summer 1998.*
Photo Gavin Bond.

BELOW: *Helena Christensen and*
*Naomi Campbell at the 'Circus'*
*collection for Spring/Summer 1997.*
*Hats by Stephen Jones; Helena's*
*corset by Mr Pearl.*
Photo Anne Deniau, 1996.

extremely well received by both buyers and press.
What it taught me was that you don't need to show
endless numbers of outfits to be commercially
successful – better to get your message across as
succinctly as possible. The third major moment of my
career was my appointment at Givenchy, and then Dior.'

What is Galliano's style? His shows are exercises
in theatrics (for his Autumn/Winter 1996–97 show,
the audience witnessed a horse's passage down the
catwalk at the start of a défilé that took its inspiration
from Native American culture and customs) and yet his
clothes are often eminently wearable once divested of
ornate styling and embellishment. 'I imagine that within
the industry I'm seen as someone who helped bring
about a return to glamour, elegance, construction and
technique, and created a revival in interest in haute
couture,' he says.

Although he may now choose to base himself in
Paris, Galliano's approach is very much that of a British
designer in that he absorbs wildly diverging historical
and cultural elements to invent new hybridizations of
the contemporary. But of course, as he himself says,
'Creativity has no nationality.'

'Drawing on the past and re-presenting it as the future, the fantasist John Galliano marries a unique romantic vision with impeccable cut and construction'

AMY DE LA HAYE, CURATOR OF 20TH CENTURY DRESS, VICTORIA AND ALBERT MUSEUM

*ABOVE AND RIGHT: Galliano for Dior Couture, Autumn/Winter 1997–98.* Photos Anne Deniau, 1997.

*OPPOSITE: Galliano for Givenchy Haute Couture: mousseline dress embroidered with a poppy motif, worn with an enamel green striped silk faille coat frogged in bronze, Autumn/Winter 1996–97.* Photo Rick Guest, 1996.

# PHILIP TREACY

Imagine a fragile sailing ship fashioned solely from chicken feathers, a hat that closes like an oyster with the face as a pearl, or a web of glowing lights curving around the head and shoulders like the tentacles of an octopus. These are the showpieces of Philip Treacy, the milliner who can transform humble ingredients into works of art. He has designed for Chanel, Helmut Lang, Versace and Ozbek, as well as for a host of celebrities in the music and fashion business; these regularly turn his catwalk show into a scrum of paparazzi and TV crews. Yet for every confection of feathers and lace, there are a dozen or more beautiful commercial pieces, such as extravagantly brimmed straw boaters and delicate white silk creations that Treacy believes will make his customer 'look great and have fun'.

'The whole point about a good hat is that it can change the geometry of your face, and there's no doubt that it can make you look more attractive,' says Treacy, whose career has gone from strength to strength since he sold his first hat, constructed from goose feathers taken from his mother's garden in Ireland.

ABOVE: *Honor Fraser models the 'Ship' hat, inspired by a 17th-century sailing ship, Spring/Summer 1995.*
Video still Nick Scott, 1996.

LEFT: *Chrystelle models a design from Autumn/Winter 1996–97.*
Photo Dee Jay.

RIGHT: *Black feather hat, worn by Michelle Paradise, 1993.*
Photo Gavin Bond.

work is at the cutting edge of millinery today. His witty and

a new fashion credibility' AMY DE LA HAYE, CURATOR OF 20TH CENTURY DRESS, VICTORIA AND ALBERT MUSEUM

Nowadays similar plumage might turn up as a coronet of peacock quills, a nifty monocle made from a ruby pheasant's tail, or decorating a simple bespoke fedora, created to fit the face of the customer. Add to these the hundreds of other hats he makes for the summer season, those for the ten couture houses in Paris, Milan and New York that he supplies, and those for the London department store Debenhams, and you realize that Treacy is not purely a showman. 'I'm really on a crusade to promote the hat,' he says. 'One of the most enjoyable parts of my work is when I get a first-time hat wearer coming to me needing something for a function and I say to them "You'll have a great time in that hat," and they look at me, puzzled. But the number of times people have come back and said, "You were right," makes it worthwhile.'

# MANOLO BLAHNIK

## 'He can even make a pair of wellies look fantastic'
LOUISE WILSON, COURSE DIRECTOR, MA FASHION, CENTRAL ST MARTINS COLLEGE OF ART AND DESIGN

A pair of 'Manolos' is the fashion byword for exquisite footwear. Fashion editors covet them; designers fight for the privilege of having them grace their runway shows. Real devotees have been known to take the Meissen off the mantelpiece and replace it with a pair of vintage heels. For despite the fact that a pair of shoes from Manolo Blahnik's Old Church Street shop may cost you a week's wages, to his supporters they are an addiction. Somehow the heels seem thinner than any others, the straps more delicate, and the foot (that most maligned part of the human anatomy) suddenly becomes an erogenous zone.

Born in the Canary Islands to a Czech father and Spanish mother, Blahnik developed his passion for footwear at an early age through the discovery of a trunk containing shoes by the Russian footwear designer Yantorny. These light-as-air creations, in brocades, silks and antique lace trimmed with buckles, were both elegant and coquettish – attributes that Blahnik later sought to match in his own creations.

Encouraged by the late Diana Vreeland of American *Vogue*, the Spanish designer settled in 1970 in London, where his exuberant footwear designs first began to create a stir. While others were producing mutations of the cork-soled platform, Blahnik, like a child in a sweetshop, started to experiment with new techniques and materials. Forget respectable; forget traditional;

Blahnik designed shoes that were sexy, not clumpy. ('He can even make a pair of wellies look fantastic,' says one long-time Manolo fan.) Suddenly, delicate blossoms appeared on narrow ankle straps, toes bore elaborate cut-outs, wet-look leather and crepe soles made their appearance in his collections. Jewel colours – not traditionally considered appropriate for the highways and byways of London – brought his customers' feet alive in shades of fuchsia, emerald and tangerine.

His philosophy remains unchanged. Every month the glossies salivate over his latest creation, whether it be a Grecian sandal designed for Galliano, with a snakelike strap that slithers up the calf, or a witty take on the traditional boating moccasin, reproportioned to form a vertiginous high heel. Wherever they are featured, Blahnik's shoes are coveted. They retain a certain theatricality that adds a fantasy element to the process of pounding the pavements. True, they are not designed for parquet floors, escalators or gardening, but who cares? He has taken the pain out of wearing high heels, and replaced it with sex appeal.

*ABOVE AND BELOW: Manolo Blahnik's sketches for designs for Autumn/Winter 1997–98.*

*BELOW LEFT: Portrait of Manolo Blahnik.*
Photo Adrian Wilson.

*OPPOSITE: Design for 1995.*
Illustration Clark Edwards.

Manolo Blahnik
.MCMXCV.

The Royal Borough of Kensington
and Chelsea

# SLOANE SQUARE SW1

KING'S
ROAD

FROM SLOANE SQUARE TO WORLD'S END, THE KING'S ROAD SYMBOLIZES A LIVING HISTORY OF BRITISH FASHION. 'IT'S ALWAYS BEEN A STREET OF PEACOCKS,' SAYS DESIGNER MARY QUANT, WHO PUT THE MILE-LONG STRETCH OF CHELSEA FIRMLY ON THE FASHION MAP IN 1955, WHEN SHE OPENED BAZAAR, THE FIRST BOUTIQUE TO OFFER AFFORDABLE DESIGNER CLOTHES GEARED SPECIFICALLY TO THE YOUNG. NEARLY FIVE DECADES LATER, SHE REMAINS A FERVENT SUPPORTER OF THE AREA, FOR ITS MIX OF THE ELEGANT AND THE TRASHY, OF EXCHANGE STUDENTS AND FIGURES THAT BELONG IN ANOTHER ERA. AND ALSO OF COURSE FOR THE PROLIFERATION OF JAPANESE TOURISTS, EAGER TO SPEND THEIR YEN IN THE TINY BOUTIQUES AT THE FURTHEST REACHES OF THE KING'S ROAD. UNLIKE SO MANY OTHER SHOPPING AREAS, THE KING'S ROAD IS A

*LIVING, BREATHING ENTITY. 'SOMEHOW PEOPLE CAN STILL AFFORD TO LIVE AROUND HERE, WHICH GIVES IT SPIRIT. SO MANY OTHER PARTS OF LONDON BECOME GHASTLY WHEN THE SHOPS SHUT,' SAYS QUANT. SHOE JUNKIES DESCEND ON PATRICK COX'S SHOP FOR ITS HAUTE-BOURGEOIS MIX OF FOOTWEAR AND ANTIQUES, WHILE MODERN-DAY COURTESANS INDULGE IN BROCADE SLIPPERS AT NEIGHBOURING DESIGNER EMMA HOPE'S SYMONS STREET OUTLET* • • • • • • • • • • • • • • • • • • • • • • • • •

**opposite:** Sloane Ranger with baby opposite Patrick Cox's shoe shop in Symons Street • • • **this page, top left:** Emma Hope shoe shop, Symons Street • • • **top right:** Sloane Ranger transport • • • • • • • **above left:** Fur coats on the King's Road – a sure sign of the foreign visitor • • • • • • • • **above right:** Outside French Connection, King's Road

AT THE DEPARTMENT STORE PETER JONES, STYLISTS FLOCK TO THE SCHOOL UNIFORM SECTION·FOR DIMINUTIVE CARDIGANS AND V-NECK SWEATERS, WHILE WELL-HEELED SLOANES CHOOSE PRE-NUPTIAL GIFTS FROM THE STORE'S FAMOUS WEDDING LIST. AT THE LOCAL SAFEWAY SUPERMARKET YOU ARE QUITE LIKELY TO BUMP INTO PAULA YATES BUYING BAKED BEANS, OR A MODEL GRABBING SOME MINERAL WATER AS SHE POPS OUT OF THE AGENCY BETWEEN APPOINTMENTS. 'WHEN I'M WANDERING DOWN THE KING'S ROAD, I CAN SEE THE WHOLE OF LIFE IN FRONT OF ME,' SAYS QUANT. 'YOU CAN BUY ANYTHING, FROM FOOD TO FASHION, ART OR ANTIQUES – IT'S A DELICIOUS MIX, MY FAVOURITE MELTING POT.' ALTHOUGH BAZAAR MAY HAVE CLOSED ITS DOORS YEARS AGO, THE POTENTIAL FASHION HISTORIAN CAN STILL DISCOVER QUANT DESIGNS AT

*STEINBERG & TOLKIEN, A CORNUCOPIA OF VINTAGE DESIGNER CLOTHING, WHICH NUMBERS THE BYGONE STARS OF BRITISH FASHION – THEA PORTER, BILL GIBB, OSSIE CLARK – AMONG ITS RAILS* • • • • • • • • • • • • • • • **opposite, left top and centre:** Outside Chelsea Register Office at Chelsea Town Hall in the King's Road – the smartest register office in London • • • • • • • **opposite, remaining photos:** Views of Antiquarius antique market, King's Road • • • • • • **this page:** Steinberg & Tolkien, purveyor of vintage clothing from the 1840s to the 1980s • • • • • • • • • • • • • • • • • • • • • • • • • • • • • • • • • • • • • • • • • • • • • • • • • • • • • • • • • • • • • • • • • • • • • • • • • • • •

IF COSTUME HISTORY IS NOT TO ONE'S TASTE, THE KING'S ROAD OFFERS THE ACCEPTABLE FACES OF GOOD TASTE IN THE GUISE OF HABITAT AND HEAL'S AND THE DAYGLO COLOURS OF DESIGNERS GUILD. FINALLY, TERENCE CONRAN'S BLUEBIRD, A COMBINATION OF RESTAURANT, DELI, FLORIST, GROCER AND KITCHENWARE EMPORIUM, IS A SYMBOL OF THE AREA'S REVITILIZATION. 'HE HAS SINGLEHANDEDLY RESURRECTED THIS AREA,' SAYS QUANT. 'AND THAT'S REALLY WHAT I LOVE ABOUT THE KING'S ROAD; IT'S A MIXTURE OF THE BEAUTIFUL AND THE TAWDRY, THE CHEAP AND THE INSPIRATIONAL — AND IT'S SO NICE TO BE IN A PART OF LONDON WHERE PEOPLE WILL STILL SAY HELLO EVEN IF I'M JUST GOING OUT TO BUY A LOAF OF BREAD.' ON THE FINAL STRETCH OF THE KING'S ROAD IS WORLD'S END, WITH ITS CURVED FACADE. BEYOND IT LIES ONE GEM:

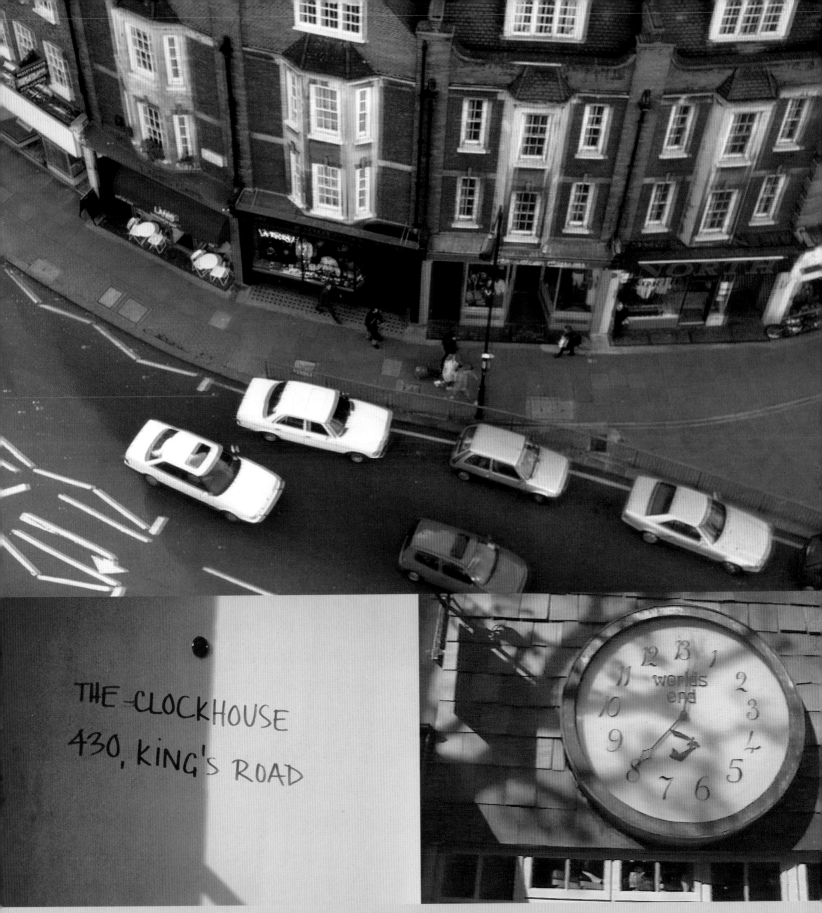

THE CLOCKHOUSE
430, KING'S ROAD

*VIVIENNE WESTWOOD'S NOTORIOUS SHOP, ALSO CALLED 'WORLD'S END', WITH ITS FAMOUS CLOCK WITH HANDS THAT GO BACKWARDS. IT IS ALWAYS BESIEGED WITH TOURISTS. AND ALWAYS, EVERY DAY, FORMER PUNKS COME TO GAZE AT WHAT HAS BECOME A SHRINE FOR SO MANY GENERATIONS* • • • • • • • • • • • • • • • • • • • • • • • •

**opposite, left column, top to bottom:** Terence Conran's Bluebird: the café, the food market and the restaurant bar • • • • • **opposite right:** King's Road doorway • • • • • •
**this page, top:** The area known as World's End, where Vivienne Westwood and Malcolm McLaren opened their shop in the early 1970s • • • • • • • **above left:** 430, King's Road, the address of the Westwood shop – one of the key locations in the history of British street style • • • • • • • **above right:** The clock outside Westwood's shop

# MODERN CLASSICS

Patrick Cox
Ben de Lisi
Nicole Farhi
Bella Freud
Katharine Hamnett
Joe Casely-Hayford
Margaret Howell
Betty Jackson
Stephen Jones
Pearce Fionda
John Rocha
Paul Smith
Amanda Wakeley

*Patrick Cox, Autumn/Winter 1997–98.*
Photo Regan Cameron, courtesy Patrick Cox.

# PAUL SMITH 'Both shops and product are intrinsically British' TIMOTHY EVEREST, TAILOR

*LEFT: Purple cashmere polo-neck sweater, Autumn/Winter 1997.* Photo Pedro White.

*OPPOSITE: Paul Smith womenswear, Spring/ Summer 1998.* Photo Mario Testino, courtesy Paul Smith Ltd. Art Direction Alan Aboud.

*BELOW: Spring/Summer 1997.* Photo Gavin Bond, courtesy Paul Smith Ltd. Art Direction Alan Aboud.

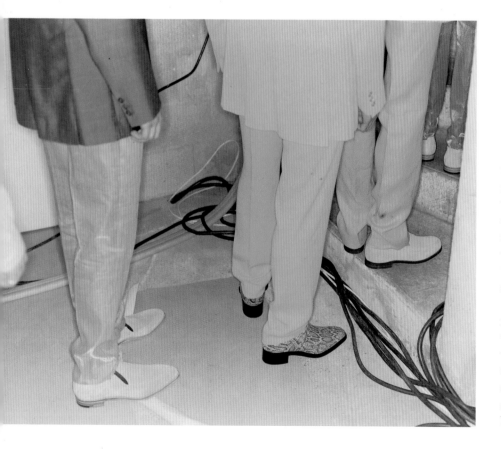

With a multimillion turnover per annum, Paul Smith is the closest thing the UK has to a Ralph Lauren or a Calvin Klein. Add to that more than 100 shops in Japan and a series of licences from childrenswear to toiletries and it is clear how far he has come since he opened his first shop in 1970 in a quiet side street in Nottingham. Today, the originator of the boxer short and the force behind the Filofax revival in the mid-1980s (a dubious accolade) is best known for his idiosyncratic approach to menswear design. Here he succeeds in blending English quirkiness with considerable commercial acumen.

In Japan he is mobbed – Beatles style – by autograph-hungry fashion students; at his Covent Garden flagship store, hoards of city boys buy armfuls of shirts on a Saturday, and if you visit any football match you will see sweatshirts and jeans emblazoned with his childlike signature. Yet, despite his huge success, Smith has managed to avoid the designer-as-popstar mentality that has been fatally attractive to others of his kind.

His very normality is his credo: 'I'm unlike other designers, many of whom work in rarefied studios and never get to meet the people who pay their wages. I have three floors in a very busy shop and I visit it every day. When you work in a commercial milieu you have to have one foot in reality.'

Whether or not his humble beginnings (the son of a draper who founded his business with a few hundred pounds) have any bearing on his public face, the shop interiors around the world reveal a lot about the Britishness of the man who 'reinvented' the four-button single-breasted suit in the mid-1980s. The Tokyo flagship store, for example, is decked out in the fittings of a Newcastle upon Tyne chocolate shop, while the Kobe outlet is fitted with a converted chemist's dispensary from Sheffield – not what you would expect from your typical designer emporium. 'I hate the fact that shops are either museums or boxes,' says Smith, 'I like the smell of polish and the feeling that somebody cares.'

Which he surely does. As the largest European menswear designer in Japan, Paul Smith has managed to increase his business over the past two decades without letting standards or perception of the brand falter. As tailor Timothy Everest explains: 'Paul Smith is a great example of someone who has kept and retained a strong identity no matter where he locates his business: both shops and product are intrinsically British.'

# JOHN ROCHA

'Mixing the traditional with the contemporary keeps so many techniques alive that would otherwise die out'

John Rocha's designs are a fusion of Oriental simplicity and Irish craftsmanship, of artistry and realism. Born in Hong Kong, of Chinese and Portuguese descent, Rocha made use of Irish linen in his London graduation show and was so inspired by the fabric that he visited Ireland and eventually settled there.

At his Dublin HQ, the focus on reinterpreting tradition is exercised judiciously. You'll always find delicate handpainted textiles and intricate embroidery in a Rocha collection, but equal emphasis is placed on cutting and tailoring and this has resulted in perennial classics such as the 'boyfriend jacket' – a short coat that is the mainstay of so many British women's wardrobes. 'Mixing the traditional with the contemporary keeps so many techniques alive that would otherwise die out,' Rocha says. 'It's not about designing clothes that would look at home at a craft fair, but about adapting some amazing techniques into modern silhouettes.'

Though he shows his womenswear collections in London and his menswear in Paris, Dublin has long been his home and base and it has a strong influence on the finished product. According to Rocha, living in Dublin removes him from the fashion milieu and allows him to design in his own way. 'If I were based in London or Paris, I would be much more influenced by streetstyle and whatever is currently in vogue. Dublin frees me from all these pressures.'

ABOVE: *Autumn/Winter 1996–97,*
Photo Dee Jay.

RIGHT: *Patsy Kensit models a jacket from the Autumn/Winter 1996–97 collection.*
Photo Dee Jay.

BELOW: *Menswear, Spring/Summer 1998.*
Photo Jean-François Carly.

# NICOLE FARHI

While so many of her kind crave the limelight, Nicole Farhi would love to become fictitious. 'It used to be great when people thought I was a brand name,' she says. 'I could get on with my life. After all, I'd rather people concentrated on the clothes than on me.' But despite her understandable reluctance to enter the public domain, her customers hanker to know more about the woman behind one of the easiest, most wearable, and most popular designer labels in the UK.

'Clothes should be like old friends,' she says, 'You put them on and feel immediately at ease.' When seen in public, she usually wears a uniform of simple trousers and a V-neck or T-shirt, but for devotees of her style there is an enormous breadth of choice, from the luxurious knitwear which feels as if it has been hand-knitted by a favourite aunt, to the simple trouser suits and warm winter coats. 'I am not the kind of designer who is inspired by foreign holidays or movies; I just update the items I really love. The only areas I won't touch are the dressy and the overtly sexy. I believe that sexiness comes from within, not through clothes.'

Farhi was awarded the 'classic' award at the British Fashion Awards in 1989 but since that time she has upgraded to the contemporary category, which she has won no fewer than three times. And the word 'contemporary' for once is apt. Neither cutting edge nor modernist, Farhi understands the needs of today's customer, and serves up her easy style by the truckload. No wonder everyone wants to know who she is.

*ABOVE: Nicole Farhi at her Autumn/Winter 1996–97 show.*
Photo Dee Jay.

'I love the idea of dropping something

on the floor in the bedroom and being able to

slip it on again next morning because

it feels so fantastic'

# JOE CASELY-HAYFORD

## 'I would find fashion very boring if I weren't having to ask myself questions the whole time'

Joe Casely-Hayford's passion for reinvention makes him a difficult designer to classify. His collections respond year after year to the fluctuations of modern society, but their roots lie in those elements of contemporary life that we all recognize: music, street people and the day-to-day movements of the city. 'I wanted to get away from the idea that clothes, especially those created by designers, are worn for reasons of status. I find that vulgar. I love the idea of free expression, rather than some kind of lifestyle aesthetic,' he says. 'Once you've got a commercially successful signature, it is easy to become complacent. I would find fashion very boring if I weren't having to ask myself questions the whole time.'

Although Casely-Hayford has more than 140 outlets around the world, most notably in the Far East, London remains his focus and the source of his inspiration. 'As a black guy living in today's society, one of the advantages you have is being able to look in – like a voyeur – on what's going on. There's an enormous variety of stimuli there – if you open yourself up to them. And I can be just as easily inspired by listening to Stravinsky as by the Wu-Tang Clan.'

The intrinsically human element in his designs extends to handcrafted touches that evoke Casely-Hayford's origins both in the rigid structure of Savile Row and in the bohemia of St Martins, the designers' alma mater. 'These give pieces a classicism that can't be mass produced,' he says. 'We've just designed some suiting in a traditional pinstripe, but it has areas of Prince-of-Wales check that have been printed onto the fabric. What appeals to me is the startling juxtaposition of a very traditional suiting fabric with a print that we've created especially for the garment.'

Despite the complex motivation behind many of his designs, Casely-Hayford's clothes are neither elitist nor obscure. In both his deconstructed shirts, buttoning to collars both at front and back, which initially brought him into the public eye in the mid-1980s, and his utility-inspired workwear which incorporated split seams and exposed linings, his task has been to recreate the created. A trouser suit becomes a skirt at the back, or a traditional Cornish smocked top is teamed with a metallic lace skirt. He is continually making hybrids of familiar items in a way that makes them appear new and fresh. 'My clothes aren't designed to make people look rich and sexy,' he says. 'What interests me is the individual, not the crowd.'

*ABOVE: Lowbrake single-breasted floral tapestry suit for Autumn/Winter 1995–96.*
Photo Zanna, 1995.

*LEFT: Black moiré anorak dress for Autumn/Winter 1996–97.*
Photo Norbert Schoerner, 1996.

*OPPOSITE: Transparent rubber double-breasted mac for Autumn/Winter 1994–95.*
Photo Marcus Tomlinson, 1994.

# PATRICK COX

'The only people left I'd like to make shoes

for are the Queen and Margaret Thatcher'

LEFT: Grey slinky satin Biba dress; grey laced anthracite peep-toe slingbacks, Autumn/Winter 1997–98.
Photo Dah Len, courtesy Patrick Cox.

ABOVE: Black satin stripe suit; grey Chinese silk print shirt; grey capretta leather slip-on shoes, Autumn/Winter 1997–98.
Photo Dah Len, courtesy Patrick Cox.

ABOVE RIGHT: Slingback design for Autumn/Winter 1997–98.
Photo courtesy Patrick Cox.

Every self-respecting fashion aficionado probably has a pair of Patrick Cox shoes tucked away in the wardrobe. Be it part of the mainline collection, the notorious Wannabe loafer, the competitively priced PC's, or even the clothing collection which echoes the understated contemporary nature of his shoes, this diminutive Canadian's designs have revolutionized the fashion footwear industry in the late 1990s. 'I originally gravitated towards shoes because they are more than just accessories, or even fashion – they exist as free-standing forms, little entities in their own right,' he says. 'And you can be a lot wilder when you're designing them.'

His passion for populism, coupled with a healthy business sense, have made Cox into a footwear guru. His work has progressed beyond the gold-knotted platforms he constructed for Vivienne Westwood in 1984 as a student straight out of college, to shops scattered around the globe and a following that ranges from wealthy socialites to students on a budget. In the hit parade of footwear, his Wannabe loafer, launched in 1993, probably rivals the Gucci loafer in terms of sales. The classic lines of this high-cut shoe with its prominent tongue attracted long queues of trendy Londoners outside his shop. 'I call them the Wannabe years,' says Cox. 'It was madness, but the biggest compliment is that they're still buying and wearing them today.'

Not satisfied with inventing one classic, in 1994 Cox launched PC's, a cheaper diffusion range of high fashion 'fun' shoes, which revitalized and repopularized the jelly sandal. 'I can remember going to visit the factory in the Brazilian rainforest, with a pocket of metal trinkets like the Eiffel tower and Big Ben which I wanted set into the heels of the sandals,' he says. 'They looked at me as if I were mad, but it worked out in the end.'

Beyond the realms of young fashion, Cox's mainline store off Sloane Square houses a further collection of offbeat classic men's footwear, and surreptitiously sexy women's shoes, displayed among well chosen antiques in an atmosphere closer to a gentleman's club than a shoe shop. 'I'm not ashamed to say I love the business side of it. When fashion allows you to be creative and make money, that's the best feeling in the world.'

ABOVE: The ultimate accessory for improving street cred: limited edition Velocifero scooter (22 made to order) customized in the UK by Patrick Cox. Cream leather upholstery with matching helmet and gold-plated wing mirrors.
Photo courtesy Patrick Cox.

BELOW: One-off boot in gold leather, worn by Tara Palmer-Tomkinson.
Photo Kevin Davies, courtesy Patrick Cox.

# PEARCE FIONDA

'They offer women who value classicism over trend a look that is current and spirited but that does not sacrifice traditional elegance' SUSANNAH FRANKEL, FASHION EDITOR, THE GUARDIAN

A column of grey silk jersey contains panels of satin that criss-cross the torso like rays of sunlight on the floor of a darkened room. It is both elegant and simple, clinging yet forgiving, and according to design duo Pearce Fionda, it epitomizes their look.

Since they first met in 1985 while studying at Nottingham Trent University, Reynold Pearce and Andrew Fionda have formed an alliance that has taken them from the brink of bankruptcy to a lucrative deal with the Debenhams department store group, for whom they create the diffusion line Pearce II Fionda, launched in July of 1997.

Their style is easy to spot: 'We believe our strengths lie in intricate bias-cutting and technically advanced tailoring that is neither tricksy nor so complex that you read the detail rather than the design,' says Fionda. The scenes in their gabled North London studio bear witness to this statement – shreds of gauzy wool lie on cutting tables like fragments of geometry, only to be transformed days later into precision-cut jackets and polished Oscar-nominee dresses.

After weeks spent scouring fabric, visiting libraries for inspiration, and working on new concepts of cut, the dénouement comes for the duo at London Fashion Week, when for twenty minutes their designs are exposed to the critical eye of the world's press. Though neither deny the importance of publicity, they know that at the end of the day, it's the product that counts. 'It's much more important for us that we're supported by the strength of our product and not by media hype,' say the boys. 'And we are no different from other designers in the pleasure we get from seeing someone wearing our designs – especially celebrities like Nicole Kidman and Helena Bonham-Carter.'

From the runaway success of their first collection for Spring/Summer 1994 ('It was the best feeling ever,' says Pearce), to a brand which is enticing younger, more fashion-literate consumers away from more traditional eveningwear houses, Pearce Fionda have been obsessed with providing the best of the three Fs (feminine, flattering and functional designs) for the consumer who wants to be contemporary rather than contrived.

ABOVE: *Hooded dress from the Spring/Summer 1998 collection.* Photo Tim Griffiths.

LEFT: *Detail of a design from Spring/Summer 1998.* Photo Jean-François Carly.

# JASPER CONRAN

## 'He does a very clever thing – making the elegant just a little dangerous' MARY QUANT, DESIGNER

Jasper Conran suffers from fashion's most pleasurable form of schizophrenia. On a visit to the theatre, you can wear his designs in the auditorium and watch them on stage at the same time. But though the theatrical costumes have been drawn by the same hand, aesthetically they're a million miles away from the simple black crepe you're wearing. 'Designing for the theatre or the ballet keeps me sane,' he says. 'I don't have to worry about whether it's commercial, or who is going to buy. It's completely unrestricted.'

With numerous ballets and theatrical productions under his belt – David Bintley's *Edward II*, staged by the Birmingham Royal Ballet in 1997, numbered no fewer than 700 costumes – Conran still finds enough time to devote to fashion to generate a multimillion turnover for his company each year.

A precocious talent, Conran has been designing since 1978, when he showed his debut collection at the age of nineteen. 'And I've never really got bored, because it's like going on a constant voyage. Each season I visit Italy to look at the fabrics and they inspire me. I love cloth and I love women; putting them together is a privilege.'

Conran's designs are enormously popular. The key to his enduring success is his respect for the women he dresses in his trademark simple columns of crepe decorated with optical prints or contrasting bands of colour, or in his deceptively simple jackets that fit sexily yet without restriction. 'Your favourite dress should be like a friend you can rely on. A lot of designers spend their time dressing dolls, which I think is demeaning. Real fashion should be for real women.'

Equally as important as the design itself is the quality of the fabrics he uses. From the affordable J range (designed in association with the Debenhams department store group since 1996) to the exclusive materials he develops in conjunction with the Italian mills for his mainline collection, the feeling of the body inside the garment is as important as the outward appearance. 'It's like a jacket in cashmere with a satin lining: the hand feels the cashmere and the nipple feels the satin.'

After two decades, Conran's collections are still greatly admired. Like his father, Terence, who revolutionized the British public's taste in home furnishings and eating out, he is obsessed by the industry of which he is a part. 'I love very simple things which will sell by the dozen, and really ornate theatrical pieces that are only for the brave. And I'm lucky enough to be able to do both.'

*LEFT:* Photo Tessa Traeger, 1992.

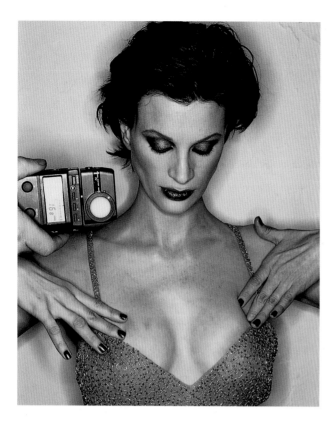

ABOVE: *Kristen McMenamy,*
*Spring/Summer 1994.*
Photo Juergen Teller, courtesy
Katharine Hamnett.

BELOW AND OPPOSITE:
*Iris Palmer, Autumn/Winter*
*1997–98.*
Photos Tim Griffiths.

Katharine Hamnett has a lot to answer for. She
popularized Habotai silk as a fashion staple in the late
1970s, got people into army-surplus-inspired gear before
it became *de rigueur*, used T-shirts for political slogans,
and became queen of the sequin at a time when it was
considered the second-rate territory of cheap eveningwear
designers. She even claims to have coined the phrase
'power dressing' in the mid-1980s ('as an expression
of power and independence which was right for the
times'). She is an original, and – despite those oh-so-
worthy tendencies that are ascribed to her – a highly
influential one.

Hamnett's other trump card is that she designs for
real people. Her clothes are neither the stuff of fantasy
nor high-street conventional: they are sexy, comfortable
and easy to wear. 'I hate the way some designers look
down on the consumer, as if once their clothes are in
the public domain it's nothing to do with them any more.
I get inspired by looking at ordinary people going about
their business, because real fashion isn't about fantasy.'

Hamnett not only oversees both men's and
womenswear collections, but also produces a highly
successful jeanswear line, footwear and even watches.
Few of her British contemporaries have their fingers in
so many pies. What's more, she still retains control of her
own company – so much so that in the design studio not
even a rivet escapes her attention.

But her hands-on approach has got her into trouble in
the past. Although at heart Hamnett is a rock chick to the
nth degree, she has won most of her headlines as a result
of her political correctness. If slogans like 'Nuclear Power
No Thanks', or '98 Per Cent Don't Want Pershing' fail to
ring a bell, you're either too young to remember, or you're
not interested in politics. 'Those silly T-shirts may have
hit the headlines, but producing them was a huge risk
for the company – they coloured the way people perceived
us,' she says. 'Nowadays I prefer to keep my moral
rectitude within the product, so we follow ethically
sound manufacturing policies, but it's unusual for us to
slogan anything. There was a rage for PVC recently, but
when we looked into it, the manufacturing process stank,
so we don't use it now.' Her political stance takes a subtler
form these days: 'When we did those T-shirts it was not
for the sake of publicity – it was because I really cared.
Nowadays it's a lot more subtle. Being ethical can be
rather cool and sexy, and not necessarily about being
a proselytizing hippie.'

'It's a youthful sexiness — aggressive yet feminine. She's as good with sequins as she is with combat trousers' BRENDA POLAN, FASHION WRITER

# AMANDA WAKELEY

## 'She understands that simple luxury speaks volumes'

HEATH BROWN, FASHION EDITOR, SATURDAY TIMES MAGAZINE

Since starting her business in 1990, Amanda Wakeley has gained fans far and wide for collections that have been described as either 'classic' or 'glamour' (she has won the British Fashion Awards in the latter category more often than any other designer).

But the secret behind her growing success is actually to do with her innate understanding of and obsession with luxury. 'There are so many clothes in the world today that frankly none of us need go out and buy another garment – ever,' she says, voicing a recurrent dilemma for contemporary designers. 'However, if something is so gorgeous that you absolutely have to have it, that's a different matter altogether.'

With its spare lines and clean, sleek silhouettes, Wakeley's brand of luxury draws on a transatlantic tradition: 'I like the American tradition because it deals in realities.' Although she is best known for updating eveningwear for a younger, more fashion-literate clientele, her easy minimalism is exemplified through small details such as Maori-inspired horn clips fastening a column of silk jersey, or one of her trademark bias-cut satin dresses, or, for that matter, her perennially popular tunics with satin cuffs. These last, though they may never see the spotlights of the runway, sell like proverbial hot cakes from her Fulham Road shop.

'Clothes are just window dressing, that's all. They needn't be expensive, but they should incorporate beautiful fabrics and brilliant fit. They're meant to flatter the wearer and make her feel confident.'

*ABOVE: Spring/Summer 1998.*
Photo Tim Griffiths.

*LEFT: Autumn/Winter 1997.*
Photo Suresh Karadia, courtesy Amanda Wakeley.

# BEN DE LISI

## 'I design what real women really want'

Given the enormous influence on British fashion of his transatlantic cousins (Donna, Ralph, Calvin and Co.), it is comforting to know that fellow-American Ben de Lisi has made it his mission to dress British women in pared-down eveningwear that may look pure Seventh Avenue but has its heart in Soho.

Since the 1970s, he has gained a steadfast following throughout the UK for eveningwear that shies away from the meringue-school aesthetic, opting instead for simple lines predominantly in silk crepe or velvet. 'I can't bear anything that looks tortured. If it's a beautiful fabric and well cut – that's enough.'

Like his Stateside counterparts, De Lisi perceives himself as unashamedly commercial, designing dresses that get to go to film premieres rather than hanging around in the showroom waiting for the next 'edgy' fashion shoot. 'I don't want to buy into that whole cutting-edge thing – everything that's shown on the catwalk is part of the selling collection,' he says.

OK, so a ticket to a De Lisi show may not be at the top of a fashion student's wish list, but in all honesty he doesn't care. 'I design what real women really want, using beautiful fabrics and simple, clean lines. You don't need to wear some kind of contraption to look good.'

For Ben de Lisi, there is no fictitious muse, just Debbie Lovejoy, his right arm, who test-drives his ideas before they are accepted into the collection. 'Nothing gets past her.' There is no target customer: 'When you see Goldie Hawn looking so fantastic in her fifties, you realize that you've got enormous scope.' And, most of all, there are no pretensions to grandeur: 'You're only as good as your last collection, and the flavour of the month isn't very appetizing when the dish has got cold.'

So, what does one expect from a De Lisi dress?

Firstly, you're wearing it, and not vice versa. Secondly, it's modern (De Lisi's favourite buzzword) and, thirdly, it looks completely effortless.

*ABOVE: Celia Chancellor, wearing a design from the Autumn/Winter 1996 collection.*
Photo © Barry Lategan.

# STEPHEN JONES

The relative calm of Stephen Jones's Covent Garden store belies the mania in the workrooms at the back. At showtime, designers queue up for confections in all imaginable materials to add the finishing touch to their collections. Whether it be a *fin-de-siècle* bonnet for Galliano, or an aggressive trilby for Andrew Groves, Jones's atelier becomes a mish-mash of wild trims and manic assistants.

Amid the hubbub, Jones himself remains tranquil. Since the beginning of the 1980s, when not working with the great and good of fashion he has made hats for everyone, from Madonna (a regular customer) to the Brazilian Fruit Board and Quaker Oats. Add to that an enormous range of custom-made pieces, plus three diffusion lines, and it becomes apparent that the dozen or so hats in the window are just the tip of a millinery iceberg.

For those whose only experience of millinery is cousin Judith's wedding, a typical Stephen Jones hat is more than just a combination of ribbon and straw. As he puts it: 'I like to think that people regard my work as a treat, more akin to chocolates or perfume than just fashion. A hat should be a pal, because it's befriending your face.'

There's an elegant humour in his work, which protects the wearer from looking ridiculous, no matter how outré the design. A typical example is a pull-on canvas boating hat, from the Miss Jones diffusion line, on which the delicately printed leaves just happen to be those of the cannabis plant. 'I put it in the collection as a bit of a joke, but none of the buyers recognized it. They just said : "Oh, what a lovely print!".'

As is the case with many of his contemporaries from the 1980s, Jones's style has been formed through a fusion of a St Martins' training and an immersion in the club culture of the time. 'While I was at college, I did a placement at the couturier Lachasse, but I was useless at sewing, so they put me to work on the hats – that's how I first became excited by millinery,' he says. With days spent in the atelier, and nights on the town in the company of serious hat wearers such as Boy George, the Stephen Jones style was born out of a combination of traditional techniques and elegant subversiveness.

Jones was, and remains, a champion of the eccentric. During his clubbing heyday, he was often seen stepping off the train, dressed as the epitome of a city banker, but with patent stilettos emerging from his immaculate turn-ups. Today he is still the most seminal British milliner. In the land of fashion hyperbole, his publicity records his qualities: idiosyncrasy, spontaneity, modernity and elegant humour – and for once, even the most sceptical critic would have to agree.

*RIGHT: Stephen Jones backstage, making final adjustments to a lace mask, at the John Galliano Autumn/Winter 1995–96 show in March 1995.*
Photo Gavin Bond.

*OPPOSITE: Trying on hats in the Stephen Jones shop in Great Queen Street at the time of the Autumn/Winter 1997–98 'Murder by Millinery' collection.*
Photo Adrian Wilson.

Today isn't like the forties, when wearing a hat

was about showing decorum'

'Though hats can serve as small pieces of cosmetic surgery,

enhancing or hiding the features, they should always be

uplifting and fun to wear'

# BETTY JACKSON

'One of the first designers to modernize knitwear

and make it a real fashion item' ANTONIO BERARDI

In a career that spans more than twenty-five years at the helm of her own company, Betty Jackson has produced clever and wearable garments that have exemplified the way modern women organize their wardrobes. Remember the casual aesthetic she pioneered in the 1980s before the widespread Lycra-ization of the UK? When British womenswear was epitomized by the tailored two-piece, she made roomy shirts, tunics and dirndl skirts a byword for effortless chic. Today, while many of her eighties contemporaries are like so much fluff in the navel of British fashion, Jackson has not lost her magic touch. 'I think the excitement in fashion lies in discovery – the shock of pleasure when you find something is different from what you expected – the feel of a fabric, or the way a garment slides onto the body. It's about practical luxury, luxury which isn't wasteful or ostentatious,' she asserts.

Although the expression 'classics with a twist' makes Jackson wince, she admits to just that. A red dress is executed in supersoft glove leather, a trademark chunky knit is teamed with a simple chiffon slip for an informal approach to eveningwear. Her studio staff rapidly absorb her aesthetic – 'It normally takes them about a month but I've had conversions in less than two days,' she says.

Jackson's customers can range in age from sixteen to seventy ('And they can even wear the same outfits because the secret lies in the interpretation'). Jackson loves the versatility inherent in her designs: 'You can wear a dress on its own, over trousers, or under a sweater,' she says, 'I think women designers always bear this in mind.'

Betty Jackson has never lost the respect of her peers, and continues to attract new devotees to her non-confrontational brand of fashion. She stands apart from the rock 'em and shock 'em school so prevalent in British fashion today, but is quietly and pervasively subversive. 'I'll keep going as long as I see the glint of desire in someone's eye when they try something on. Without that, fashion becomes just clothing.'

*RIGHT: Coat from the Autumn/Winter 1997–98 collection.*
Photo Dee Jay.

# MARGARET HOWELL

## 'I love a slight eccentricity in the character of the wearer'

A string of handmade papier-mâché beads started it all back in 1969. Now Margaret Howell has a retail presence in Japan that is second only to Paul Smith ('We're always bumping into each other in the hotel swimming pool when we're in Tokyo on business') and she is the figurehead of one of the best loved, yet lowest-profile fashion companies in the UK.

In the early 1970s she singlehandedly reinvented the white cotton shirt, transforming it from the stuffy cliché of the bowler-hatted English businessman into a softer, more modern, silhouette. She has spearheaded a movement towards androgyny, dressing modern-day farm girls in boilersuits, slouch pants and droopy masculine jackets. Though she claims not to love British fashion as such, she is attracted to the 'quintessential' British style found in tweed, Irish linen, pinstripe wools and cotton gaberdine, and to the traditional craftsmanship and quality seen in British tailoring and in such items as the English raincoat.

Beyond her interpretations of the classics lies a certain quirkiness which can be glimpsed in her mismatched silhouettes and incongruous blends of fabric. 'I'm attracted to the work of architects like Edward Lutyens and Norman Foster, or people like Katharine Hepburn and Alan Bennett. I love a slight eccentricity in the character of the wearer,' she says.

She is not obsessed with those vagaries of fashion that demand a certain palette or hemline every season. Prior to her Spring/Summer 1998 show she decided to blend in old pieces from previous collections to give continuity to her designs. 'I love clothes with a history, that have been worn and cherished. Nobody wears brand-new garments from head to toe, and I wanted to reflect that kind of realism in the show.' This same realism belies a sophistication of design that has made Howell's work a staple for men and women throughout the country.

*LEFT: Reefer coat and white cotton drill wide-legged trousers, Autumn/Winter 1997–98. Photo Alistair Taylor-Young.*

*BELOW: Iris Palmer wearing grey wide-legged wool trousers and stretch paisley shirt, Autumn/Winter, 1997–98. Photo Alistair Taylor-Young.*

# BELLA FREUD

In the echelons of designers, Bella Freud lies somewhere in the twilight world that separates the established 'Old Guard' and the 'New Generation'. Her designs are clever, amusing and flirtatious, yet never edgy; her philosophy is simple, and her approach intrinsically British.

'I love messing about with proportion and fit', she says. 'For instance, you can take a Victorian silhouette, and play with its dimensions without disguising its roots, so that it remains sexy in a repressed way, because the design centres on what you show, even if it's only an ankle or wrist.'

'When I started in 1990 there was nobody doing tailoring that was young or lighthearted; it was all either very classic or experimental,' says Freud. 'I wanted to offer the younger woman something that fell between youthful charm and dandyism, but which didn't make her look as if she had walked out of a costume museum.'

Her trademark fitted knits can curve over the bosom and bottom, while her tailoring adds a dandyish edge to the subtlest silhouette. Freud has reinvented many classic garments using contemporary techniques.

Although she claims her family connections are irrelevant – 'My father (painter Lucian Freud) designed the dog's head trademark that is my logo, but that's about it' – she uses colour and texture very much as a painter would. Her passions are pastels and chalky bright shades far removed from the E-number colours that personify so many of today's wardrobes.

*ABOVE: Astrakhan jacket worn with velvet trousers, Autumn/Winter 1996–97. In the background is a painting by Lucian Freud, the designer's father, part of an exhibition of his work held at the Abbot Hall Gallery, Kendal.* Photo John Swannell, courtesy *Country Life.*

*RIGHT: At the end of the show, London Fashion Week, Autumn/Winter 1997–98.* Photo Tim Griffiths.

*OPPOSITE PAGE: Tufted fake-fur coat, satin trousers, polo top, Autumn/Winter, 1996–97.* Photo John Swannell, courtesy *Country Life.*

elegantly kinky and flirtatiously witty' LUCILLE LEWIN, OWNER OF WHISTLES

COVENT
GARDEN

*'Covent Garden is like an exotic fruit cocktail. Every ingredient has a different origin. As you walk through the area you know that each passer-by has his or her own outlook on life, and this diversity is what gives the area its special character and spirit.'* LUCILLE LEWIN, OWNER OF WHISTLES

LUCILLE LEWIN, OWNER OF WHISTLES, THE HIGH FASHION CHAIN OF SHOPS, IS FASCINATED BY COVENT GARDEN. AND THAT'S NOT JUST BECAUSE HER STORE IN THE PIAZZA TAKES MORE MONEY THAN ANY OF HER OTHER BRANCHES, BUT BECAUSE THE AREA HAS AN IDENTITY THAT'S IMPOSSIBLE TO DEFINE • • • • • • • • • • • • • • • • • • • • 'WHEN I FIRST ARRIVED IN THE UK AT THE BEGINNING OF THE SEVENTIES, COVENT GARDEN WAS NO MORE THAN AN ANTIQUATED FRUIT AND VEG MARKET. NOW IT'S THE ONE PLACE IN LONDON THAT REINVENTS ITSELF FROM WEEK TO WEEK' • • • • • • • • • • • • • • • • • • • • • • • • • • • • • • • • • • • • • • FOR LEWIN, THE AREA IS A SHIFTING MASS OF THE FASHIONABLE AND TOURISTY, THE URBAN AND URBANE, AND THE DOWNRIGHT TACKY. 'IT'S ONE OF THE BEST PLACES IN

LONDON TO WANDER AIMLESSLY AND INDULGE IN A SPOT OF PEOPLE WATCHING,' SHE CLAIMS. 'YOU'LL SEE HOARDS OF TOURISTS WITH BIG CAMERAS WHO FLOCK TO WATCH THE STREET PERFORMERS, SKATEBOARDERS WITH PIERCINGS, AND TWENTYSOMETHING URBANITES READY TO FLEX THEIR CREDIT CARDS IN ANY ONE OF A HUNDRED SHOPS'

**this page and opposite:** Covent Garden habitués

AND YET, ACCORDING TO LEWIN, THE SHEER DIVERSITY OF THE AREA HAS MADE ITS PERSONALITY DIFFICULT TO CLASSIFY: IT IS A THOROUGHFARE FOR THOSE WHO WANT TO SPEND, TO GAWP OR TO GRAB A QUICK MEAL BEFORE MOVING ELSEWHERE • • • • • • • • • • • • • • • • • • 'I REALLY CAN'T DEFINE ITS NATURE. SOMETIMES IT'S EXTREMELY FASHIONABLE, SOMETIMES BEST AVOIDED, BUT ALWAYS BUSY' • • • • • • • • • • • • • • FOR LEWIN, AND MILLIONS OF OTHER VISITORS, AN AFTERNOON SPENT IN THE VICINITY INEVITABLY INVOLVES SPENDING MONEY. FOR, UNLIKE THE NEIGHBOURING WEST END, IT IS A CURIOSITY SHOP OF SORTS, WHERE THE AVID CONSUMER CAN BUY ANYTHING FROM A SHARP SUIT AT PAUL SMITH ON FLORAL STREET, TO DRIED FISH ROE AT CARLUCCIO'S ITALIAN DELI • • • • • • • • • • • • • • • • • 'I CAN SPEND HOURS SHOPPING HERE,'

SAYS LEWIN. 'I MAY STOP IN AT SPACE NK APOTHECARY, BECAUSE IT HAS SUCH AN AMAZING RANGE OF MERCHANDISE, FROM OBSCURE BEAUTY PRODUCTS TO NAIL FILES

WITH REAL DIAMOND CHIPS, OR I'LL MAKE A BEELINE FOR NEAL'S YARD DAIRY, WHICH HAS A MOIST, CAVE-LIKE ATMOSPHERE AND IS FILLED WITH WONDERFUL CHEESES —

IT'S AN AMAZING ENVIRONMENT' • • • • • • • • • • • • • • • • • • • • • • • • • • • • • • • • • • • • • • • • • • • • • • • • • • • • • •

**above:** The Paul Smith shop, Floral Street • • • • • • • • • • • • • • • • • • • • • • • • • • • • • • • • • • • • • • • • • • • • • • • • • •

• • • • • • • • • • • • • • • • • • • • • • • • • • • • • • • • • • • • • • • • • • • • • • • • • • • • • • • • • • • • • • • • • • •

FOR THE CLOTHES SHOPPER, THERE'S EVEN MORE TO WHET THE APPETITE. AS A CLOTHING RETAILER HERSELF, LEWIN ADMITS TO A CERTAIN BIAS, YET ADMIRES THE WORK OF

PAUL SEXTON AND TALITA ZOE AT KOH SAMUI, WHICH CHAMPIONS YOUNG AND EXPERIMENTAL DESIGN ('IN A WAY THEY SYMBOLIZE COVENT GARDEN BECAUSE THEY ARE

YOUNG, INNOVATIVE AND CONSTANTLY CHANGING'), AND VINTAGE CLOTHIER CENCI, ON MONMOUTH STREET, WHERE JAYNE MANSFIELD-STYLE TWINSETS AND FIFTIES SKI

JUMPERS NESTLE IN A RETRO ATMOSPHERE. AND AS FOR MENSWEAR, THERE'S NO STOPPING THE MODERN-DAY PEACOCK WITH CASH TO SPEND. 'EVERYONE KNOWS ABOUT

PAUL SMITH, BUT THERE'S ALSO SLAM CITY (SKATEBOARDING), BURRO (GOOFY), JONES (DESIGNER), DUFFER OF ST GEORGE (STREET) AND JIGSAW (CONTEMPORARY) — IT'S A

POTENTIAL NIGHTMARE IF YOU'RE NOT SURE WHAT YOU'RE AFTER. I'D IMAGINE YOU COULD EASILY SPEND FAR MORE THAN YOU ANTICIPATED,' SHE LAUGHS. LAST, BUT NOT

LEAST, IS WILD BUNCH, THE SPRAWLING PAVEMENT FLORIST AT SEVEN DIALS, WHERE YOU'RE JUST AS LIKELY TO FIND ORCHIDS AND PROTEAS AS TULIPS AND DAFFODILS. IT'S

A FAVOURITE OF LEWIN'S, FOR WHOM FLOWERS REPRESENT THE ULTIMATE IN EVERYDAY LUXURY. 'WILD BUNCH <u>IS</u> COVENT GARDEN TO ME. AND, LIKE WILD BUNCH, COVENT

GARDEN IS A MIXTURE OF THE EVERYDAY AND THE EXOTIC. LIKE THE BUCKETS OF FLOWERS, IT BUDS, BLOOMS AND WILTS, ONLY TO BE REPLACED WITH A FRESH BUNCH THE

FOLLOWING DAY' · · · · · · · · · · · · · · · · · · **left and above:** Covent Garden, daytime and night-time · · · · · · · · · · · · · · · · · · · · · · · · · · · · · · · · · · · · · · · ·

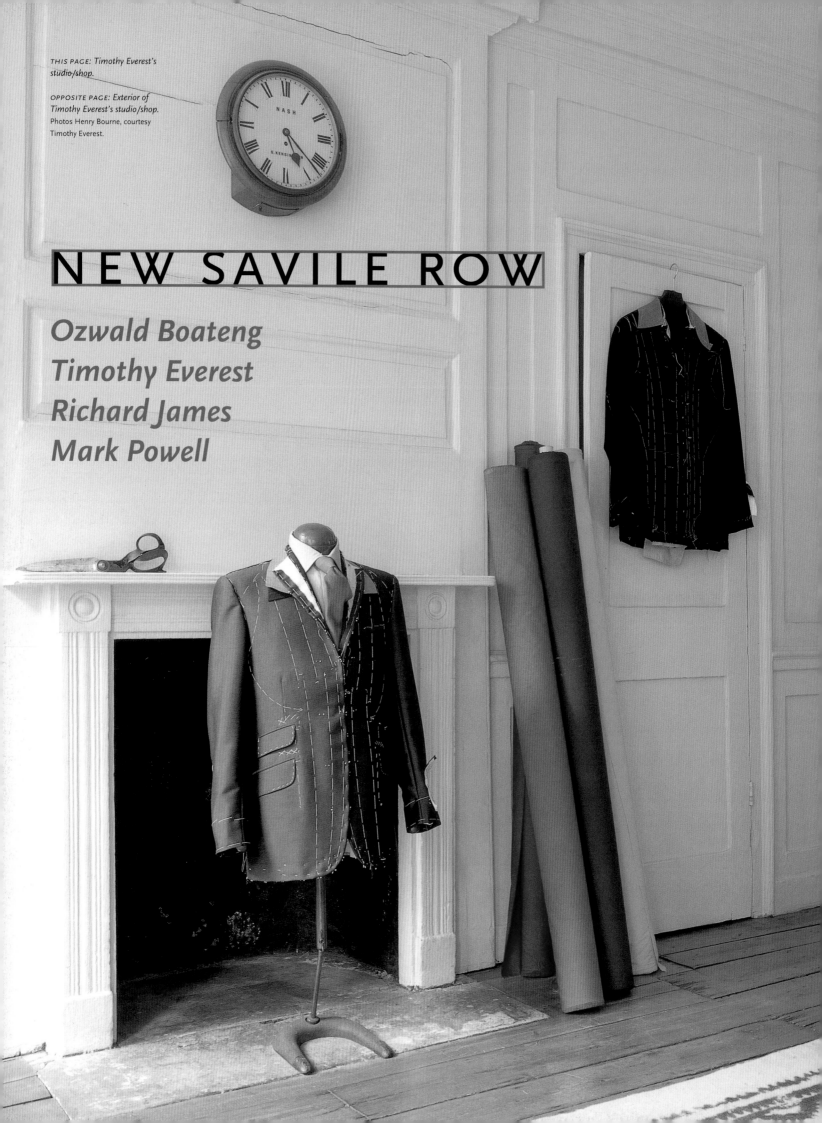

THIS PAGE: *Timothy Everest's studio/shop.*

OPPOSITE PAGE: *Exterior of Timothy Everest's studio/shop.* Photos Henry Bourne, courtesy Timothy Everest.

# NEW SAVILE ROW

**Ozwald Boateng**
**Timothy Everest**
**Richard James**
**Mark Powell**

# RICHARD JAMES  'An incredible perennial talent:

## Cecil Beaton meets David Hockney meets Jean Cocteau in

## brilliantly ingenious menswear' RICHARD MARTIN, CURATOR, THE COSTUME INSTITUTE, THE METROPOLITAN MUSEUM OF ART

At Richard James's shop, the brightly lit interior, vases of exotic flowers and the slow chant of reggae in the background belies what is still essentially a traditionally run establishment. 'People consider us mad when we say we're traditionalists,' James says, 'but the jackets we produce conform to the typical Savile Row shape, that is, a soft shoulder, longer silhouette and a slightly fitted waist. What's different about us is that we've attracted a younger customer by using more adventurous materials.' And it is true that the exuberant colours and unusual fabrics employed by James have brought a new wave of customers to Savile Row, where the traditional bespoke tailors are only just beginning to get used to the idea that a handmade suit may not be solely the territory of the ageing captain of industry.

So among the traditional monotone suiting fabrics in James's shop are bales of cloth more suited to a candy store than a Savile Row establishment, including a jade green tweed which has just been transformed into a jacket for American designer Isaac Mizrahi, and a roll of what looks at first glance like traditional chalkstripe wool but turns out to have a rainbow thread. 'Designers like Paul Smith made it acceptable for men to wear colour and we enable them to continue making that choice,' says James. 'Nowadays it's perfectly O.K. for men to wear moisturizer, and there are so many men's style magazines on the market that today's bespoke customer has a broader perspective on fashion.'

Catering for a gamut of famous names that include Elton John and Christian Lacroix does not exclude the 'young creative professional' who forms the mainstay of James's clientele. 'We may have a celebrity following but we're not so grand that we don't listen to what our customers need,' he says. 'Bespoke translates as "bespoken for" – something that's made especially for you – and to get this type of product right, everybody has to have hands-on attention.'

RIGHT: *Savile Row, London 1996. Ozwald Boateng is sitting on the pillar box. To the right of him is Timothy Everest and to the left Richard James. The models on the right are wearing Timothy Everest outfits; those on the left are dressed by Richard James. Boateng's establishment is just around the corner, in Vigo Street.* Photo Michael Roberts.

'Timothy  Everest  breathes  new  life  into

Savile  Row  with  every  stitch' RICHARD MARTIN, CURATOR, THE COSTUME INSTITUTE, THE METROPOLITAN MUSEUM OF ART

The interior of Timothy Everest's atelier, situated in a Huguenot townhouse in Spitalfields (an area better known for its sweatshops than for bespoke tailoring), has a tranquillity that is misleading. For although the butter-coloured wainscots and battered sofas may exude an olde worlde charm, the product – in bold checks, bright silks and quirky tweeds – is anything but conventional. Dubbed the baby boomers' favourite, Everest has a pedigree that qualifies him as a member of 'New Savile Row' despite the fact that he has chosen to locate himself a stone's throw from a street of curry houses. 'One of the differences between us and some of the other younger tailors is that we have elected not to be in Savile Row itself. Our customers usually find us through word of mouth and we try to get everyone sitting together and having a chat. It's very relaxed,' he says.

There is no aspect of Everest's life that has not been coloured by bespoke: his great uncle was a tailor; he himself trained under the legendary sixties tailor Tommy Nutter and at twenty-four was designing suits for Elton John's World Tour – complete with shoulder pads that Alexis Colby would have given her eye teeth for. Today, he is at the forefront of a tailoring style that he sums up as 'very structured, very patterned, very masculine – it's about an exaggerated Savile Row cut teamed with a witty use of colour and pattern.'

Although most of his output may still be in grey, a typical example of a Timothy Everest suit would be of pin-haired, window-pane or bouclé fabric with a purple Bemberg lining, which combine to form a single-breasted three-button jacket and flat-fronted trouser with a narrow leg. 'Everything about it would be slightly narrower than the norm,' he explains.

Ask who his clients are and he suddenly becomes evasive. 'I'm very old-fashioned in that I believe that a tailor shouldn't divulge that kind of information.' But, needless to say, they're a mixture of politicians and businessmen and a smattering of pop stars and celebrities – not forgetting the baby boomers, who, like so many New Savile Row customers have turned to bespoke after a surfeit of designer dressing in the late eighties and early nineties. 'They've come to us because there is something very passé about an over-the-top catwalk number,' he claims.

Everest's dream of getting his contemporaries interested in something he had believed was a dying art has made him obsessed with proving the relevance of bespoke at the end of the century. And with outlets for his ready-to-wear lines in New York and Japan as well as in London, it looks as if his dedication is bearing fruit.

# MARK POWELL

'Mark Powell and Ozwald Boateng draw on the rich heritage and

techniques while offering garments that speak today's language

For Mark Powell, Soho's Carnaby Street has had as much influence on his work as the wood-panelled ateliers in Savile Row, on the other side of Regent Street. 'I feel there is as much history in men's tailoring here in Newburgh Street (behind Carnaby Street) as there is in Savile Row, especially since World War II, when a new generation of European tailors challenged the typical Englishman's silhouette.'

Like Galliano, Powell has a passion for basing his designs on historical reinterpretation. 'Much of what I design has elements of nostalgia,' he says. He is known for his signature Edwardian gangster suits, which have become an integral aspect of his house style. 'Most people associate me with a high-buttoned jacket, with three to four covered buttons, probably a top flap pocket with turn-back cuffs and an inverted pleat at the back. This would be worn with flat-fronted trousers with a full cut leg.'

Although bespoke's new kids on the block have brought Savile Row back into the limelight since the 1980s, Powell is fatalistic about the future of the craft of tailoring. 'The first Savile Row tailors were Jewish immigrants, but their children chose not to pursue the tradition. They were followed by Greek Cypriots, but their sons took up professional careers as well. Ten years down the line there will be problems, because the expertise won't be there any more.'

Despite this gloomy projection, the great and good of the media and music industry are much in evidence at Powell's Newburgh Street atelier, as also are women, who make up between a quarter and a third of his business (Naomi Campbell orders five or six suits at a time). Powell ascribes this popularity with women customers to the expertise a bespoke tailor can bring to whatever shape of torso submits to his tape measure.

'Ultimately,' he says, 'the best thing about this job is spotting people wearing my designs. And although a lot of tailors copy the detailing, they don't pay as much attention to the finish as I do. I like to think that those in the know will remember my influence and that, like other avant-garde designers, I'll at least get a footnote in history.'

ABOVE: *Mark Powell tailoring.*
Photo Patrizio Di Renzo, 1996.

# OZWALD BOATENG

mpeccable reputation of Savile Row

n terms of colour and shape' DAMIAN SHAW, MENSWEAR BUYER, LIBERTY

In his bright tweeds and dark shades, the elegant Ozwald Boateng is by far the least retiring and most fashion oriented of the new Savile Row tailors and he has done much to raise the profile of British tailoring. While his contemporaries are content to work discreetly in their cutting rooms, Boateng is busy showing his elegantly crafted suits in Paris during the menswear catwalk shows, or perfecting his latest advertising video which features 'people who look as if I went to school with them and who have now grown up to wear my designs.' He has also launched a capsule collection of womenswear, which debuted during London Fashion Week in October 1997.

His dandified suits typically have a long, slim silhouette, and, like his contemporaries, he uses a multicoloured tweed as often as a grey flannel. 'A bespoke suit is the equivalent of couture for a man, and yet it's a fraction of the cost. So why not be experimental?', he says, in a workroom that could easily pass as a Parisian atelier.

With dreams of making Savile Row – the street of suits – into the menswear equivalent of a couture house, Boateng's wish is to create an environment where bespoke tailoring is perceived as a modern artform. 'If Dior and Valentino can do it, I don't see why we can't. The men's suiting market is one of the biggest in the world, so why shouldn't the British bespoke industry try to be like Bill Gates (at Microsoft) and show that handmade tailoring is an essential luxury for everyone?'

Boateng's lack of traditionalism makes him the least typical of his contemporaries. He takes the traditional fitted suit shape that typifies Savile Row and stretches it: 'I'm not afraid to try the new, and a longer silhouette is a modernization of a traditional block that looks right for the nineties,' he asserts.

'Bespoke tailoring is about having a strong, conscious awareness of form and how it relates to the body. Men have very different requirements from those they had twenty years ago,' he says. 'What we are doing today is creating menswear for the new millennium.'

*ABOVE AND RIGHT: Stills from a video made for Ozwald Boateng in 1996. The shot below is part of a sequence in which Boateng is being pursued by various people who have been hired by a traditional Savile Row tailor who wishes to discover the secret of Boateng's success. Suit from the Autumn/Winter 1996–97 collection.*
Video direction Trevor Robinson, through Jane Fuller Associates, courtesy of Ozwald Boateng Ltd.

SOHO CONJURES UP A DIFFERENT IMAGE IN EVERYONE'S MIND: DEN OF INIQUITY, GAY PARADISE, CHEAP FRUIT AND VEG, OR EVEN CLIFF RICHARD STRUMMING A GUITAR IN

A CAPPUCCINO BAR. ALL THESE (EXCEPT POSSIBLY THE LATTER) HAVE CONTRIBUTED TO AND STILL COLOUR OUR PERCEPTIONS OF THE BUZZING SQUARE MILE THAT MAKES UP

THE CORE OF LONDON'S CLUB AND STREET FASHION SCENE. AT THE MARKET IN BERWICK STREET, WHERE LONDON'S WEST END BUYS ITS FRESH PRODUCE, THE SELLERS TRY

VAINLY TO COMPETE WITH THE BEAT OF MUSIC EMANATING FROM THE ADJACENT RECORD SHOPS. IT IS MORNING, AND BOY/GIRL DJ DUSTY 'O', SHATTERED FROM A NIGHT

SPINNING DISCS AT A POPULAR SOHO NITERIE, PICKS UP SOME VEGETABLES FROM A STALLHOLDER AND A COUPLE OF METRES OF SATIN FROM ONE OF THE MANY FABRIC

*'I can't hear the cry "Three for a pound!" without thinking of Berwick Street Market. It's an organic thoroughfare in the heart of a ghetto, and the sight of all the produce in among the endless traffic and exhaust fumes is refreshing and uplifting' – DUSTY 'O'*

*SHOPS THAT ARE KEPT AFLOAT BY THE PROXIMITY OF STUDENTS FROM ST MARTINS AND THE LONDON COLLEGE OF FASHION. SOHO, HE DECIDES, IS EXHAUSTING, FROM THE WORN-OUT PROSTITUTE ENTICING MYOPIC BUSINESSMEN TO EXPERIENCE A 'LOVE SHOW' AT A LESS THAN SALUBRIOUS CLUB, TO THE CHEAP ITALIAN AND CHINESE RESTAURANTS WHERE YOU CAN EAT FOR A FIVER, IT CATERS FOR EVERYMAN AND NO MAN* • • • • • • • • • • • • • • • • • • • • • • • • • • • • •

**both pages:** Views of Berwick Street and its market • • • • • • • • • • • • • • • • • • • • • • • • • • • • • • • • • • • • • • • • • • • • • • • • •

FOR DJ DUSTY 'O', SOHO IS FRAGMENTED INTO AS MANY DIFFERENT ASPECTS AS THE AREA'S LONG HISTORY. AFTER A NIGHT BEHIND THE DJ CONSOLE, HE CAN FLOP DOWN IN FULL DRAG AND DRINK AN ESPRESSO WITHOUT ANYONE BATTING AN EYELID. 'IT'S THE ONE AREA IN LONDON WHERE I CAN GO AROUND WEARING A FULL VIVIENNE WESTWOOD OUTFIT, AND PEOPLE ARE MORE LIKELY TO SAY "HELLO, YOU LOOK FANTASTIC," THAN WANT TO SHOVE A BOTTLE IN YOUR FACE,' HE SAYS • • • • • • • • • • • • • • • • • • • • • • • • • • • • • • • • • • • • • • • • • • • • • BY MIDDAY, A NEW BREED OF PASSER-BY FILLS THE STREETS. TRENDY EURO TOURISTS TAKE A BREAK FROM THEIR SHOPPING AT ANY ONE OF THE NUMEROUS COFFEE BARS AND RESTAURANTS, WHILE COUPLES OF VARYING SEXUAL

'Old Compton Street is the Champs-Elysées of Soho, where you can hang out in a coffee bar and watch the world go by. What better way to spend an afternoon than over a cappuccino with such ready entertainment on your doorstep?' – DUSTY 'O'

*ORIENTATION FLIRT ACROSS THE PAVEMENTS, OR HOLD HANDS WITHOUT RISKING PREJUDICE* • • • • • • • • • • • • • • • • • • • • • •

• • • • • • • • • • • • • • • • • • • • • • • • • • • • • • • • • • • • • • • • • **opposite top**

**left:** Freedom Café Bar, Wardour Street • • • • • • • • • • • • **opposite top right:** La Crêperie, Old Compton Street

**opposite centre:** Costa coffee bar, Broadwick Street • • • • • • • **opposite bottom right:** Cigarette break, Berwick Street

**above:** Pavement café, Old Compton Street • • • • • • • • • • • •

'For cards and birthday presents I go to American Retro, and for jewelry – ranging from the kitsch to the exquisite – I drop into Janet Fitch.

I shop at Kokon to Zai for clothes – amazing and obscure Japanese imports that you can't buy anywhere else in London.

Soho is a pleasure palace and everything for sale there is surplus to requirement' – DUSTY 'O'

LIKE EVERY DRAG ARTISTE, DUSTY'S FAVOURITE PASTIME IS SHOPPING. HE IS THINKING OF HAVING A HAIRCUT (IT NEEDS TO BE KEPT SHORT UNDER A BLOND WIG), BUT THE BLUE DREADLOCKS AND PIERCING OFFERED IN THE SALON AT DANIEL POOLE SEEM A BIT DRASTIC, AND THE TACKY CHARM OF 'BOY' AT THE FURTHEST END OF OLD COMPTON STREET FAILS TO FURNISH THE PECULIAR SHADE OF EYESHADOW THAT IS REQUIRED TO MATCH TONIGHT'S DIOR SUIT – BETTER TRY 'LIBERTY', IF HE CAN COPE WITH THE THRONGS OF TEENAGE EXCHANGE STUDENTS IN CARNABY STREET. AFTER YET ANOTHER COFFEE (SOHO IS FUELLED BY CAPPUCCINO), HE BUYS A HYSTERIC GLAMOUR T-SHIRT FROM 'SHOP' ON BREWER STREET, AND, WHILE STROLLING UP TO SOHO SQUARE FOR A SPOT OF SUN, DROPS INTO 'KOKON TO ZAI' ON GREEK STREET, TO BROWSE THROUGH

DOZENS OF OBSCURE EUROPEAN TECHNO RELEASES, WHILE WONDERING WHO ON EARTH WOULD PAY £100 FOR A PAIR OF WOODEN JAPANESE CLOGS DISPLAYED IN ITS STARK WHITE INTERIOR • • • • **opposite top left:** Dusty 'O' in Vivienne Westwood suit, shopping in Berwick Street • • • • **top centre:** Kokon to Zai, Greek Street • • • • • • **opposite bottom left:** Outside Boy, Old Compton Street • • • • **opposite centre right:** Dusty 'O', inside Boy • • • • **opposite bottom right:** Vexed Generation, Berwick Street, producer of fashionable but environmentally friendly clothes • • • • **this page, top right:** American Retro (kitsch emporium), Old Compton Street • • • • **this page, bottom right:** Shop, Brewer Street, one of Soho's best clothing stores • • • • • • • • • • **this page, above:** A satisfied customer leaves Agent Provocateur, Broadwick Street

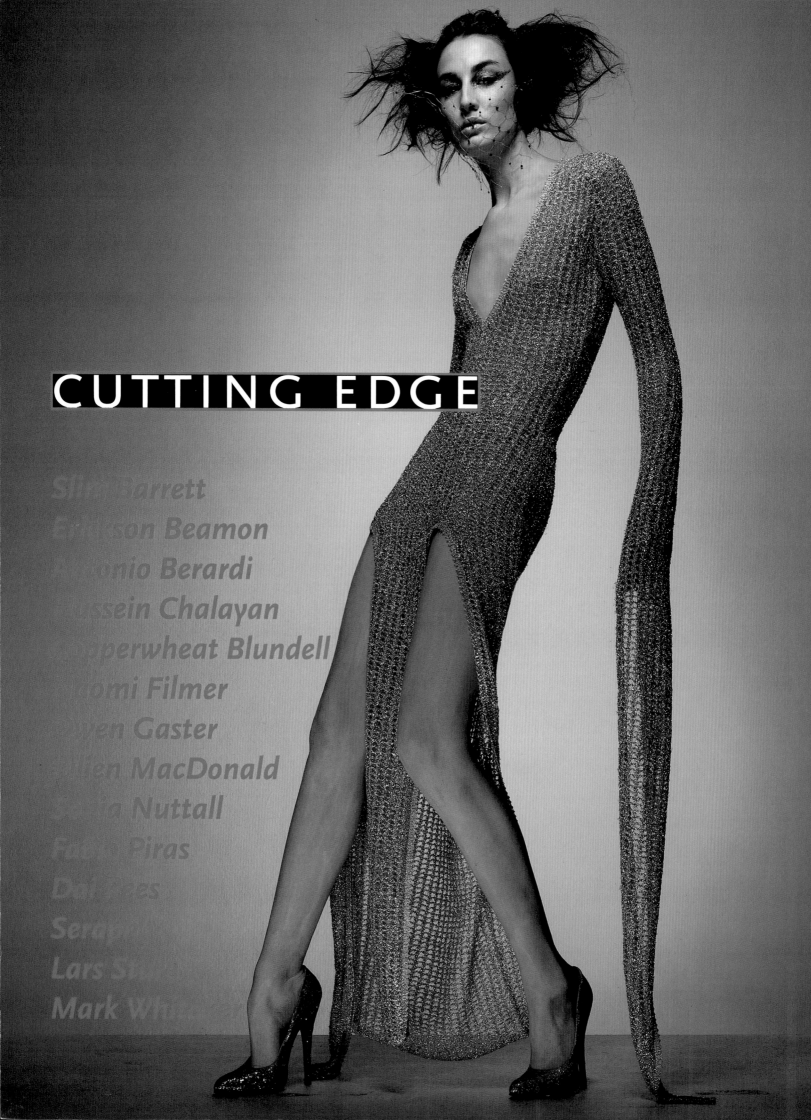

# CUTTING EDGE

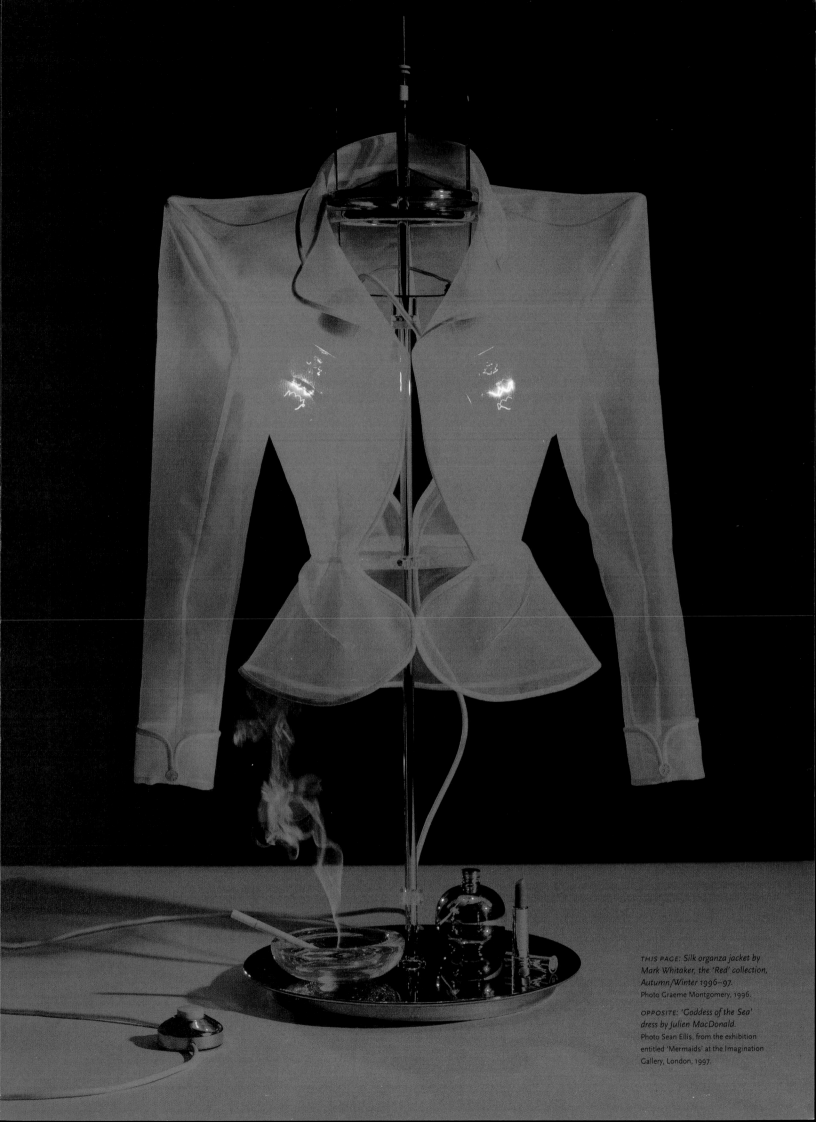

THIS PAGE: *Silk organza jacket by Mark Whitaker, the 'Red' collection, Autumn/Winter 1996–97.* Photo Graeme Montgomery, 1996.

OPPOSITE: *'Goddess of the Sea' dress by Julien MacDonald.* Photo Sean Ellis, from the exhibition entitled 'Mermaids' at the Imagination Gallery, London, 1997.

# ANTONIO BERARDI

'The reality is that he produces

eminently wearable clothes'

ANGELA QUAINTRELL, BUYER, LIBERTY

Antonio Berardi's swift ascent into the forefront of contemporary British fashion left his contemporaries speechless. For in the hostile environment that surrounds the passage from graduate to designer, he has led a charmed life. In 1994 this former Galliano assistant stole the limelight at his St Martins graduation show by commissioning a scent from the same fragrance house as Calvin Klein as a gift to the bemused press. Four years later, no fewer than a dozen design houses were pleading with him to reinvigorate their names. Today he is celebrated for a sense of design centring around pastiche and historical reinterpretation, combined with elements of contemporary culture.

For his debut collection of September 1995, Berardi combined subway art with delicate *fin-de-siècle* cutting and fabrics in a combination of nineteenth-century poise and Ragga decoration. In his Autumn/Winter 1997 collection, models with dishevelled hair and dirty faces appeared like genies from clouds of smoke to the accompaniment of voodoo drums. They wore clothes that signified a fusion of the piratical and the modern.

Berardi's signature designs mix Galliano with a heady dose of British street style. A dress may be painstakingly embroidered, beaded, smocked and handpainted (often all four techniques are employed) but it has more to do with reality than with merely catering for some fictitious muse. Consider for instance his Spring/Summer 1998 show, which took place in the sleazy charm of the Brixton Academy under a sign spelling out the designer's name in fairground lights. Opening the show, Naomi Campbell sashayed down the runway in a dress constructed of white bobbin lace which had taken fourteen Sicilian women three months to make. Yet, despite the workmanship, the garment possessed a realism that lifted it above the trite reinterpretation of costume. Berardi may understand that fashion demands the pomp and circumstance of a big performance, but his intention is to make the fantastic as accessible as possible.

RIGHT: *Antonio Berardi makes an adjustment to his slashed PVC jacket for his Autumn/Winter 1997–98 collection. The jacket is worn with a wool pleated skirt.* Photo Anders Overgaard, 1997.

# COPPERWHEAT BLUNDELL

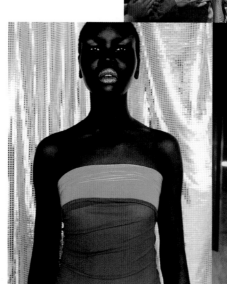

When so few designers resemble the clothes they create (imagine Karl Lagerfeld wearing Chanel), design partners Lee Copperwheat and Pam Blundell are the best advertisement for their own label because they create with themselves in mind, steering more towards casual and sportswear ideas than anything too wacky.

What is obvious to the casual observer is that both designers are products of their environment: hence the distinctive style of the clothes, which are both modern and urban. Anyone familiar with the *fin-de-siècle* London street scene will recognize elements of it in Copperwheat Blundell designs.

In their Spitalfields studio, the duo have devised a technique where they work in tandem on every aspect of building the collection, from fabric and colour to pricing and the correct finishes. They have evolved together for such a long time that they understand each other's taste – a fact that is apparent to anyone who knows their designs, which get slicker each season as key styles are refined and reinterpreted. They do not feel the need to change direction every season; if they themselves want to carry on wearing something, they simply offer a newer version in the next collection. As Copperwheat puts it: 'We're designing for a lifestyle, not a fantasy.'

TOP: *Pamela Blundell and Lee Copperwheat acknowledging the applause at the end of their Spring/Summer 1998 show.* Photo Tim Griffiths.

ABOVE LEFT: *Alex Wek, wearing an orange, purple and blue net layer dress for Spring/Summer 1997.* Photo Kim Andreolli/Sygma.

ABOVE: *Ben from the band Catch wears a grey stretch herring-bone suit from the Autumn/Winter 1997–98 collection.* Photo Rankin.

# FABIO PIRAS

Stark, sombre, bleak – not terms one usually associates with fashion, but in Fabio Piras's case, the darker elements inherent in his work are all-defining.

Piras's style exemplifies the cultural diversity of London: the son of Sardinian parents, educated in Switzerland and based in the East End – all these factors are reflected in his designs. 'People ascribe a lot of romanticism to Sardinia, but life is tough there, and when I moved to Switzerland I was struck by how pristine and efficient it was,' he says. In his clothes he contrasts the Swiss elements of simplicity and clean lines with the poverty of his native island through a mix of uncluttered shapes executed in basic fabrics such as cotton poplin, wool, twill and denim, using a mainly dark palette of grey and the inevitable black.

Despite the gloomy approach, however, Piras's garments manage to be challenging without being difficult, and beautiful without being ostentatious. Dresses are draped across the body, often breaking the severity of hard, almost cuboid cutting. Proportions are manipulated, skirts may have deep waistbands that stand away from the torso, while stiff, boiled-wool tops and dresses have an ecclesiastical structure, reminiscent of cassocks and ceremonial robes. 'There's a kind of restrictive sexuality in a lot of the cutting; it's very much a man's image of how a woman should look, but without the misogyny of so many other designers,' Piras says.

His London roots are, he feels, integral to the evolution of his design, but he is keen to distance himself from the hype that appears daily in the media. 'London is like a vampire, it absorbs everything, drains its energy and leaves things to be reborn in different guises. It's a process of decay and regeneration.'

While his womenswear may relate to the harshness of rural life in Sardinia, Piras's menswear collection is a more personal, almost egocentric vision. 'I design for myself – it's autobiographical,' he says. To understand his philosophy, it helps to look at Piras the man. His thin frame and pianist's hands reflect a sombre aesthetic that relies on sparsely cut garments in rough, functional fabrics which make the wearer look like a refugee or a consumptive from the pages of a romantic novel.

But though Piras has a bleak vision of the future, though his muses are gaunt, his fabrics basic and his silhouette simple, beneath all the angst are surprisingly easy, wearable clothes. If being cruel to be kind typifies a new approach to fashion, Piras is in the vanguard.

*ABOVE: The collection for Spring/Summer 1998 is based on Melody Nelson, the fictional character created by the French composer Serge Gainsbourg. It portrays the exotic and erotic adventures of a child/woman. Photo Tim Griffiths.*

*ABOVE RIGHT: Spring/Summer 1998. Photo Jean-François Carly.*

*RIGHT: Spring/Summer 1998. Nail Art Design: The Untouchables and K-Sa-Ra. Photo Jean-François Carly.*

*BELOW: Fabio Piras with his models at the end of the Spring/Summer 1998 show. Photo Tim Griffiths.*

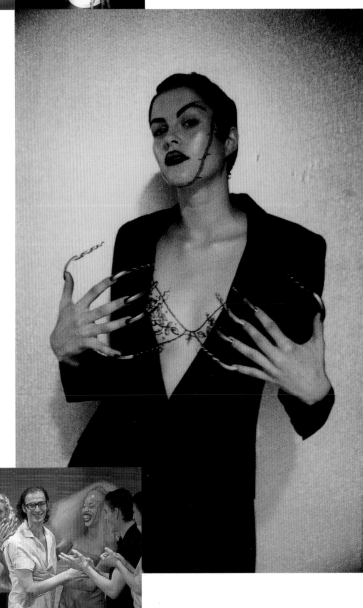

# HUSSEIN CHALAYAN

'I look at the role of the body in different cultural contexts, such as architecture, science or nature, and see how these approaches can be applied to clothing'

From conceptualization to finished product, the process has been a long one for Hussein Chalayan. It started with some buried jackets covered in particles of rust at his 1993 St Martins degree show (the models were obliged to have anti-tetanus injections before appearing) and has forged him a reputation as a designer who challenges traditional concepts of how fashion is derived.

Minimal without being vacant, modern without being contrived, Chalayan's designs have origins that might not immediately be apparent to the bystander. 'I look at the role of the body in different cultural contexts, such as architecture, science or nature, and see how these approaches can be applied to clothing,' he says.

Typically, in his Autumn/Winter 1997 collection Chalayan explored the way we ritualize the weather so that it takes on symbolic meaning. To the audience at this show, the inferences were so subtle that the message was conveyed almost subconsciously. Ceremonial beaded veils evoked Islam, yet with a fragility that suggested droplets of water; fitted capes suggested protection from a storm. But the overall effect was one of beautiful garments with a basis in something too complex for immediate definition. 'What inspires me is capturing the gap that lies just between fantasy and reality,' explains Chalayan.

To his detractors, buried garments coated with iron filings, glowing mouthpieces, and paper suiting inset with illuminated flight paths are seen as gimmicks rather than serious messages. To his supporters, Chalayan's clothes are modern and wearable. But whether you go to a Chalayan show looking for an intellectual challenge or searching for beautiful clothes, you will always leave satisfied.

ABOVE: 'Scent of Tempests' collection, Autumn/Winter 1997–98. Photo Daffyd Jones.

LEFT: Paper coat, from the 'Along False Equator' collection, Autumn/Winter 1995–96. Photo Gavin Bond.

OPPOSITE: 'Between', Spring/Summer 1998. Photo Dee Jay.

'More than any other fashion designer with the possible exception of Rei Kawakubo, Chalayan uses clothing as an art to reinterpret and reform the human body in a continuous *tour de force* of body/identity conceptualism and dressmaking' RICHARD MARTIN, CURATOR, THE COSTUME INSTITUTE, THE METROPOLITAN MUSEUM OF ART

# MARK WHITAKER

## 'I think of my work as pleasurably shocking'

Mark Whitaker's career move from fashion editor on the US men's style magazine *Details* to fashion designer in the humbler climes of an atelier in Clerkenwell has given him the freedom to explore his own creative identity. 'Journalism often meant that you were having to do fifty things at once. It's such a luxury to be able to shut myself up in the studio for three days and get on with what I really want to do,' he says.

The eclectic influences that inspire his clothing have produced massively diverse collections. His debut, entitled 'Red', for Autumn/Winter 1996–97, focused on a capsule range of waspish tailoring interpreted in vivid carmine (see page 107). His collection 'Black' for Spring/Summer 1997 was shown on Afro-Caribbean models and offered architectural black leather pieces that were slashed and cut to expose the flesh beneath. 'Soft', for Autumn/Winter 1997–98, gently transformed the wearers into giant marshmallows of tactile pastel fabrics.

'Each season I design a collection that reflects a different part of me, so that I don't get pigeonholed as a designer who can only do one thing. Eventually I see all these ideas as running parallel so that people can choose what looks they want from an ongoing series. I want to produce items that are well crafted but that aren't dress-makers' pieces and to avoid becoming some kind of all-encompassing empire. I think of my work as pleasurably shocking: challenging, but beautiful to wear.'

*LEFT: Silk taffeta gown, 'Print' collection, Spring/Summer 1998. Photo Tim Griffiths.*

*BELOW: 'Print' collection, Spring/Summer 1998. Photo Dafydd Jones, 1997.*

*OPPOSITE: Wool tweed cape from the 'Soft' collection, Autumn/Winter 1997–98. Photo Ram & Fab.*

# SONJA NUTTALL

Sonja Nuttall's life is full of what she calls 'pared-down moments' – those times of day when she shuts out the superfluous and concentrates on honing her designs down to their bare minimum in pursuit of perfection. She may be pigeonholed with much of the angry young talent that constitutes cutting-edge British design, but her capacity for 'getting things right' has more to do with deceptively easy design than with creating a frisson among her audience. She describes herself as 'massively anally retentive'. 'We spend hours in the studio playing with cut, fit and length, and at the end of the day the only difference in a trouser may be a few millimetres – but to me they make all the difference.'

Constantly dubbed 'the British Jil Sander', Nuttall employs gentle, almost ergonomic cutting which replaces the frills and frou-frou so prevalent in much of today's fashion. A wardrobe of Nuttall classics would include a plain boiled-wool frock coat, slouch trousers, a loose tunic with a simple cut neck, and a classic boyish suit – all designed with the wearer, not the media, in mind. 'Actually, though people think I'm a purist, there is nothing that I wouldn't design. Everything I do boils down to interpretation: the biggest challenge would be to turn a garment with traditionally vulgar associations into something miraculous,' she says.

Since her first collection in Autumn 1994, she has gained a steadfast following of women who choose to protect, rather than flaunt, their individuality. 'At the end of the day, I want to create clothes that reinforce the wearer's sense of identity. It's more to do with the brain than the body.'

*ABOVE: Sonja Nuttall at work in her studio with her muse, Rebecca Lowthorpe.*
Photo Martyn Thompson.

*LEFT: Model on the catwalk at the Spring/Summer 1998 show.*
Photo Dee Jay.

# SERAPH

Seraph clothes are what the fashion crowd love to describe as 'edgy' (read 'innovative'). Raw, hand-bleached denim jackets combine with delicate net blouses sprinkled with patches of diamanté. The overall effect is dynamic – a mixture of the challenging and the easily adaptable, a blend which designer Sherald Lamden sees as integral to the label's handwriting. 'I want people to understand that you can mix both fantasy and reality in a collection.'

Lamden's background is central to her approach to design. She had worked on a consultancy basis for a range of designers, most latterly with Ghost, which provided the impetus and initial finance for the Seraph label to spread its wings. 'Working with everyone from rag-trade wholesalers through to Ghost taught me more than just business. Designers like Galliano cater

for a fantasy, whereas someone like Armani is a strict realist – I thought, 'Why not combine the two elements?'

Seraph has evolved into a label which in many ways typifies urban London of the late nineties. Lamden explains: 'My parents are from India, and I grew up in a working-class area of North London, where many of my friends came from massively different cultural backgrounds. The whole concept of what is British mutates in an environment like this; our heritage isn't necessarily European, but our nationality is, and the mixing leads to a hybridization of culture.'

These diverse influences appear in her clothes. There are flavours of Hassidic Jewish, Asian and Afro-Caribbean cultures, yet with an interpretation so subtle that each nuance looks fresh rather than contrived.

*BELOW: Autumn/Winter 1997–98.*
Photo Mark Mattock.

'I want people to understand that you can mix both fantasy and reality in a collection'

## 'Our fortes are cut, fabric and detailing'

*LEFT AND RIGHT: Designs for 'Fiend', the Spring/Summer 1998 collection, inspired by Ragga.*

*Left: Blue lurex pedal-pusher suit.*

*Right: Frock coat and trousers. The trousers are made in an original Dior check.*
*Gold jewelry also by Owen Gaster.*
Photos Peter Robathan.
Styling Seta Niland. Hair Barnabé.
Make-up Miriam Langelotti.

'We cut a mean trouser,' says Owen Gaster, with a modesty that belies the cleverness of his technical skills, which include such tricks as starlike seams and armour-like cutting.

Gaster manages to achieve a balance between being perceived as an avant-garde designer and as one whose garments have a cut and structure which make them eminently wearable. 'When you see the catwalk show', he points out, 'the cut and detail are lost on the audience, but the message behind the collection remains very strong.' And though the shows may include heat-sensitive plastic bodices, jumbo asymmetrical bobbed wigs, and models with hands weighted with sovereign rings, the key pieces are in fact the intricately tailored jackets and the low-cut trousers with hidden seams and clever proportions. 'I want people to look interesting,' says Gaster, and to this end he provides a kind of quirkiness that never slides into parody.

'While drawing

on Britain's

tailoring tradition,

Owen Gaster is a

modernist offering

youthful and

experimental

designs – often

in daring new

materials'

AMY DE LA HAYE,
CURATOR OF 20TH CENTURY DRESS,
VICTORIA AND ALBERT MUSEUM

# AGENT PROVOCATEUR

## 'Actually we get very few weirdos'

JOSEPH CORRE, CO-FOUNDER, AGENT PROVOCATEUR

A female lawyer has just snapped up a mint suspender belt with fuchsia lace trim, while at the till a smart, thirty-something woman in a suit has spent a small fortune on a selection of bras in various colours and sizes. 'I think she's a bra designer for Marks & Spencer,' explains the assistant, as she wraps a pink 'Bunny' bikini overlaid with polka-dot tulle for a well-known model. Yes, it's just another typical morning at Agent Provocateur, Soho's premier purveyor of glamorous lingerie.

Founders Joseph Corre and Serena Rees are relaxed about the company's success, for since 1994, when they opened their doors on Broadwick Street, a loyal clientele has learnt the joys of shopping for exotic lingerie designed to make the wearer feel sexy rather than furtive. 'Shopping for a bra in a lot of department stores is no more exciting than buying a loaf of bread,' says Corre, 'and there's nothing erotic about buying lingerie in an environment where nylon g-strings are displayed next to a rack of porno mags.'

ABOVE: Joseph Corre, co-founder of Agent Provocateur and son of Vivienne Westwood, photographed inside the shop in Broadwick Street, Soho.
Photo Polly Borland/Sygma.

RIGHT: Leopard-print panties.
Photo Sean Ellis, The Knicker Shoot, 1995.

OPPOSITE: Black baby-doll dress by Agent Provocateur.
Photo Rankin, Fake, 1996.

True, it may be Soho, but the ambience inside Agent Provocateur is more inclined to that of a turn-of-the-century Parisian brothel than a cut-price sex emporium. You can lounge on a lipstick velvet chair as ornate Chinese lanterns cast a faint glow through a carmine and turquoise interior, or you can slip into a little something behind rose-printed chiffon draperies. 'It was almost a political decision to go into business,' says Corre. 'Ten years of Thatcherism had bred such an atmosphere of uniformity in our shops, yet Soho's "gay village" had a really sexual, carnival-like feel. We wanted to create something with a similar flavour, which offered choice and value in quality and content.'

Not only is it intimate and special, but Agent Provocateur contains a range of products that would make sexual icons like Betty Page and Mata Hari flex their credit cards to breaking point. Corre and Rees scour Europe and the USA for items that put more commercial shops to shame, yet all the time encouraging their clientele to treat lingerie buying as a form of self-pampering whether the purchase is a simple pair of knickers or a vintage fifties bra. As the name suggests, Agent Provocateur is not your typical lingerie retailer. You won't get arrested if you buy a bra, but you'll leave feeling just a little bit naughty.

# JULIEN MACDONALD

'He is reinventing knitwear
in a youthful, wearable
way for a new generation'

SUZY MENKES, FASHION WRITER, INTERNATIONAL HERALD TRIBUNE

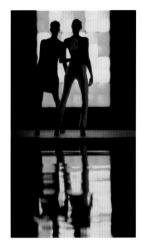

ABOVE: *Spring/Summer 1998.*
Photo Dee Jay.

His sylph-like creations resemble the stuff of daydreams, so why should we be surprised to discover that Julien MacDonald's meteoric rise to success has been no less than a modern-day fairytale? One minute a struggling Royal College of Art student, the next the toast of Paris as designer Karl Lagerfeld flouted convention by bringing his twenty-five-year-old protégé out onto the catwalk to be scrutinized by the world's press at the finale of his Autumn/Winter 1997 show. Subsequently dubbed 'the maestro of the knitting machine', this young man from Merthyr in South Wales has crocheted his way into another dimension.

MacDonald has a passion for knitwear, and an understanding of technique that has conjured exquisite creations from the type of knitting machine that normally accumulates dust in the back of someone's garage. Ocean green lurex is crocheted into a fine symmetrical spider's web; layers of gold and silver filigree evoke ancient lace; and synthetic threads resembling fishing tackle are combined with the finest cashmere. These are dresses so delicate they look like museum pieces, yet they are small and supple enough to be rolled up into a ball and stuffed in a handbag. 'It's all

to do with technique', says MacDonald, 'and the fact that you can break the limitations of traditional knitting if you're brave enough. Knitwear design today has only been limited because people don't fully understand what amazing things you can do with a ball of wool.'

Working with Lagerfeld at Chanel has taught the fledgling designer a lot about the commercial limitations of the fashion industry (his knitted tweeds were some of the best-selling designs in the Autumn/Winter 1997 collection), yet it has also allowed him to create items of breathtaking ingenuity, such as his filigree work in metallic threads for the house's couture collection.

MacDonald's own designs are flights of fancy, plundering mythical images of mermaids imagined while on a childhood holiday, combined with a healthy appreciation of a woman's sexuality. 'Everyone considers my work delicate. I don't dispute that, but my ideal customer is an older woman who's comfortable with her looks and not afraid to show off her body. I'm only happy when what I design evokes a passion in the wearer. It's about putting something on and loving it in a way you can't define because each garment has its own history.'

OPPOSITE: *Lara Belmont, wearing a polyamide knit dress with bird-of-paradise feathers, from the 'Mermaids' collection, Autumn/Winter 1997–98.*
Photo Sean Ellis from the exhibition at the Imagination Gallery.

RIGHT: *Jodie Kidd, wearing a gold suit-of-armour dress with antique embroidery from the 'Modernist' collection, Spring/Summer 1998, held at Spitalfields Market, Commercial Street, E1.*
Photo Sean Ellis.

# SLIM BARRETT
# ERICKSON BEAMON
# NAOMI FILMER
# DAI REES
# LARS STURE

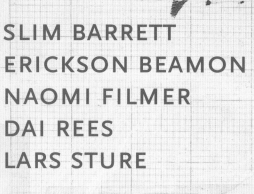

Although nobody will deny that 'a diamond is forever', contemporary British jewelry design has less to do with representing eternal romance than with manipulating the body and challenging concepts of personal adornment.

True, young British jewelers are not averse to a spot of the real stuff (in 1997 Slim Barrett created a tiara containing over £250,000 worth of gold and diamonds) but the ornate beaded jewelry that made Erickson Beamon famous is usually paste, and a headpiece by Dai Rees may be fashioned from nothing more precious than the bare quills of feathers found on the banks of the pond in London's Finsbury Park.

What concepts lie behind the creations and what are their links with contemporary design? For jeweler Naomi Filmer, who shot to prominence when Hussein Chalayan's models sported her glowing tonsils and metallic fangs in his collections for 1996 and 1996–97, the inspiration behind her ideas centres on new manipulations of the body: 'My main concern is focusing on the negative spaces in and around the body, such as illuminating the mouth, or placing a ring *between* the fingers, not around them. It's about creating anonymous objects that fall into context when placed on the body,' she says.

Slim Barrett, who is self-taught and proud of it, says: 'Traditional jewelers are trapped in technique. This prevents them from exploring new relationships with their product and leads to boring design.' Barrett proclaims his versatility as a designer through a repertoire which spans both the delicate tiaras so beloved by the party set and the cruder 'wing mirror' headpieces created for Galliano's collection of Spring/Summer 1997. Likewise, Norwegian designer Lars Sture can switch his talents from supremely commercial earstuds like tiny sea urchins ('they're dull to make but sell really well') to high-gothic leather and jet gauntlets and collars for Fabio Piras's Autumn/Winter 97–98 collection. 'Working with designers allows me to expand my ideas beyond the confines of what most people consider jewelry to be,' he says. And this symbiosis has pushed the role of the contemporary jeweler way beyond the engagement ring market.

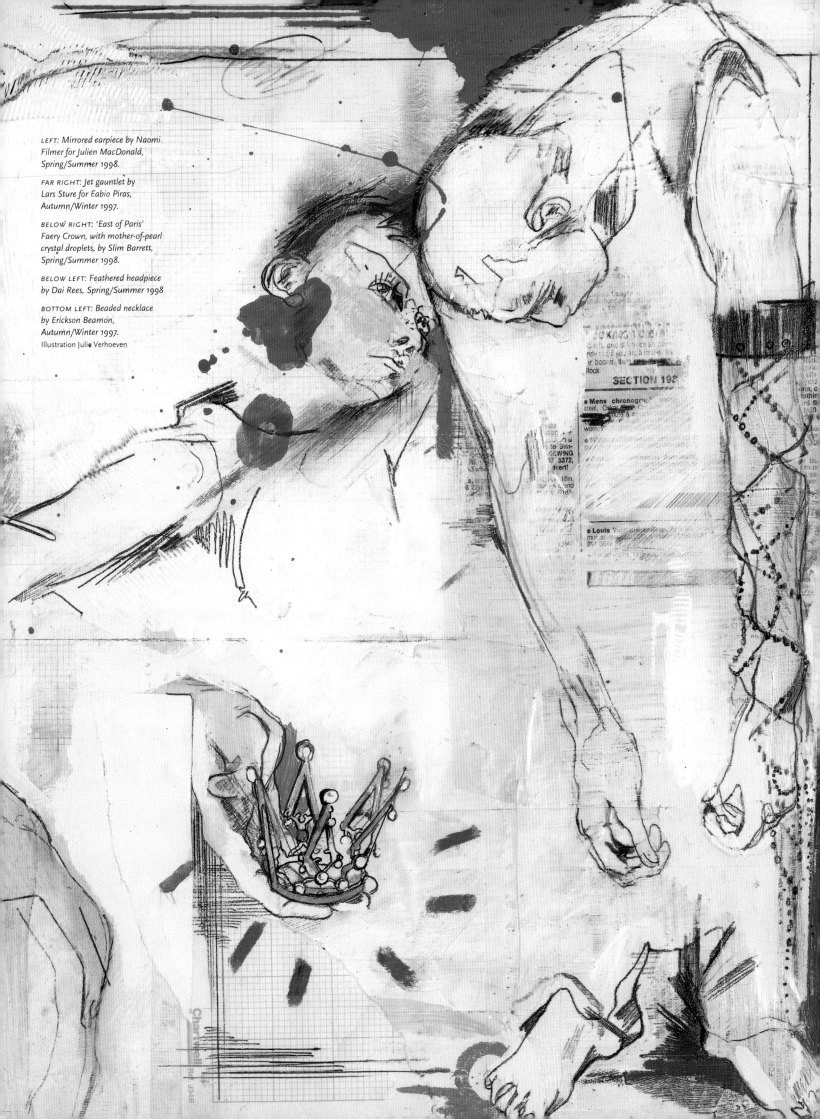

LEFT: *Mirrored earpiece by Naomi Filmer for Julien MacDonald, Spring/Summer 1998.*

FAR RIGHT: *Jet gauntlet by Lars Sture for Fabio Piras, Autumn/Winter 1997.*

BELOW RIGHT: *'East of Paris' Faery Crown, with mother-of-pearl crystal droplets, by Slim Barrett, Spring/Summer 1998.*

BELOW LEFT: *Feathered headpiece by Dai Rees, Spring/Summer 1998*

BOTTOM LEFT: *Beaded necklace by Erickson Beamon, Autumn/Winter 1997.*

Illustration Julie Verhoeven

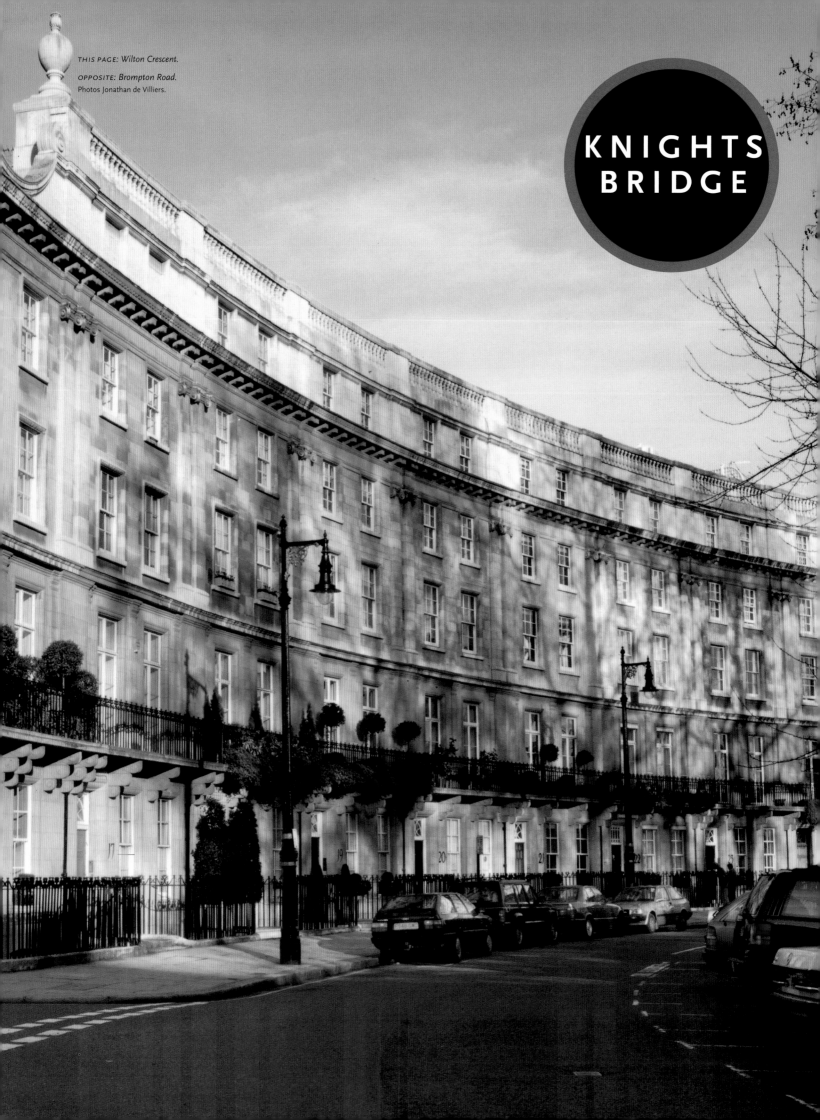

# KNIGHTS BRIDGE

CAUGHT ON ONE OF HER MANY SHOPPING FORAYS AT JOSEPH, TARA PALMER-TOMKINSON, IT GIRL EXTRAORDINAIRE, PAUSES TO CONSIDER WHAT MAKES KNIGHTSBRIDGE HER SECOND HOME. SHE HESITATES FOR A MOMENT, THEN, 'GLAMOUR, GLAMOUR AND MORE GLAMOUR,' SHE STATES. AND SHE'S RIGHT. THIS AREA MAY NOT HAVE THE STREET THEATRE OF COVENT GARDEN OR THE CHAOTIC VARIETY OF NOTTING HILL GATE, BUT ITS BLUE-CHIP CHARM MAKES IT AN INTERESTING AND ENGAGING DESTINATION. FOR BEHIND DEPARTMENT STORES HARRODS AND HARVEY NICHOLS ARE NUMEROUS SHOPS THAT TRANSCEND THE NOTION OF ANONYMOUS CHIC. AT THE LIBRARY, BROMPTON CROSS, YOU CAN FIND THE RIGHT BOOKS TO COMPLEMENT THE RIGHT SUIT, AND AT EGG, IN KINNERTON MEWS, MAUREEN DOCHERTY, THE OWNER,

'I love the villagey feeling that exists behind the madness of the Brompton Road' – TARA PALMER -TOMKINSON

WILL QUITE HAPPILY PULL UP A CHAIR AND CHAT WHILE HER SHOP IS BESIEGED BY MOVIE STARS AND BUYERS FROM THE USA, WHO HAVE STOPPED BY TO INVESTIGATE THIS TINY CONVERTED GARAGE IN A QUIET COBBLED LANE. ONCE YOU'VE HAD YOUR FILL OF EGG'S HANDCRAFTED TEXTILES AND DECEPTIVELY SIMPLE OBJETS D'ART, SELINA BLOW'S ATELIER ON ELIZABETH STREET OFFERS A DAYGLO FEAST OF BROCADE AND VELVET AND, FOR THE MORE EXPERIMENTAL, TOKIO, AGAIN AT BROMPTON CROSS, SELLS A HOST OF UNUSUAL AND CUTTING-EDGE DESIGNER LABELS • • • • • • • • • • • • **opposite:** Tara Palmer-Tomkinson in Joseph • • • • • • • • • • • • • • • • • • • • • • • • • • • • • • • • • • • • •
**this page, clockwise from top left:** The Library, Brompton Road; Egg, Kinnerton Street; Tokio, Brompton Road; Selina Blow in her shop in Elizabeth Street • • • • • • • • • • • •

BUT WHILE TARA MAY FAVOUR GUCCI, PRADA AND DOLCE & GABBANA AS HER STORES OF CHOICE, THE BACKBONE OF THE AREA IS ITS ENGLISHNESS. HOME-GROWN

SOPHISTICATES INCLUDE ANYA HINDMARCH, WHOSE ELEGANT HANDBAGS, ON SALE IN HER SHOP IN PONT STREET, ARE THE FIRST CHOICE OF YOUNG THOROUGHBREDS

• • • • • • • • • • • JO MALONE, CREATOR OF HANDCRAFTED FRAGRANCES • • • • • • • • • • • • • • • • • • • • • • • • • • PHILIP TREACY, MAKER OF ELABORATE CONFECTIONS OF FEATHERS • •

• • • • • • • • • • • • • • • • • • • • • • • • • AND ERICKSON BEAMON, KNOWN FOR THEIR ELEGANT COSTUME JEWELRY • • • • • • • • • • • • • • • • • • • • • • • • • •

IN THE GINA WINDOW IN SLOANE STREET, YOU WILL FIND A PAIR OF EXTRAORDINARY SEQUINED BOOTS WHICH CATCH THE ATTENTION OF EVERY PASSER-BY AND WHICH

*EPITOMIZE THAT COMBINATION OF QUALITY AND DESIGN SKILLS FOR WHICH THIS FAMILY-RUN BUSINESS IS FAMOUS • • • • • • • • • • • • • • • • • • • • • • • • • • • •*

**opposite, clockwise from top left:** Anya Hindmarch, Pont Street • • • Jo Malone, Walton Street • • • Erickson Beamon, Elizabeth Street • • • Philip Treacy, Elizabeth Street

**above:** Gina, Sloane Street • • • • • • • • • • • • • • • • • • • • • • • • • • • • • • • • • • • • • • • • • • • • • • •

AS WITH ANY SHOPPING MECCA, KNIGHTSBRIDGE PROVIDES ITS DISCERNING CUSTOMERS WITH A VARIETY OF WATERING HOLES IN WHICH TO RELAX • • • • • • • • • • • •

TARA PALMER-TOMKINSON IS OFTEN SPOTTED WITH A COFFEE AND STICKY BUN AT HER FAVOURITE HANGOUT IN WALTON STREET, AND YOU'RE JUST AS LIKELY TO SHARE A

TABLE WITH A DOWAGER DUCHESS AS A SECRETARY IN THE GLORIETTE PATISSERIE IN BROMPTON ROAD • • • • • • • • • • • • • • • • • • • • • • LATER, AFTER A TRIP TO THE

HAIRDRESSER, OR A PERIOD OF QUIET CONTEMPLATION AT THE SLOANE CLUB, THE RITES OF SHOPPING BEGIN AGAIN • • • • • • • • • • • • • • • • • • MORE SHOES AT

GINA, AND A POSSIBLE VISIT TO JIMMY CHOO SEEM IN ORDER • • • • • • • • • • • • • • •

*KNIGHTSBRIDGE HAS EVERYTHING FROM THE COSMOPOLITAN TO THE HOME-GROWN • • • • • • • • • • • • • • • • • • • • • THE SHOPPING THERE MAY BE THE ULTIMATE IN*

*SELF-INDULGENCE, BUT DON'T EXPECT IT TO COME CHEAP • • • • • • • • • • • • • • • • • • • • • • • • • • • • • • • • • • • • • • • • • • • • • • • • • • • • • • •*

**opposite:** Gloriette Patisserie, Brompton Road • • • • • • • • • • • • • • • • • • • • • • • **this page, left top and left centre:** Gianni and Claudi, hairdressing salon, Motcomb Street

**top centre and centre:** The Sloane Club, Lower Sloane Street • • • • • • • • • • • • • • • • • • • • • **top right:** Gina, Sloane Street • • • • • • • • • • • • • • • • • • • • •

**above left:** Gloriette Patisserie, Brompton Road • • • • • • • • • • • • • • • • • • • • • **above right:** Jimmy Choo shoe shop, Motcomb Street • • • • • • • • • • • • • • •

# THE THOROUGHBREDS

THIS PAGE: *Tomasz Starzewski:*
*Red dress, with lacework over*
*fabric; skirt in quilted satin.*
OPPOSITE: *Bruce Oldfield: Black*
*and white satin patchwork dress*
*with a double bodice; under-bodice*
*in red.*
Illustrations Camilla Dixon.

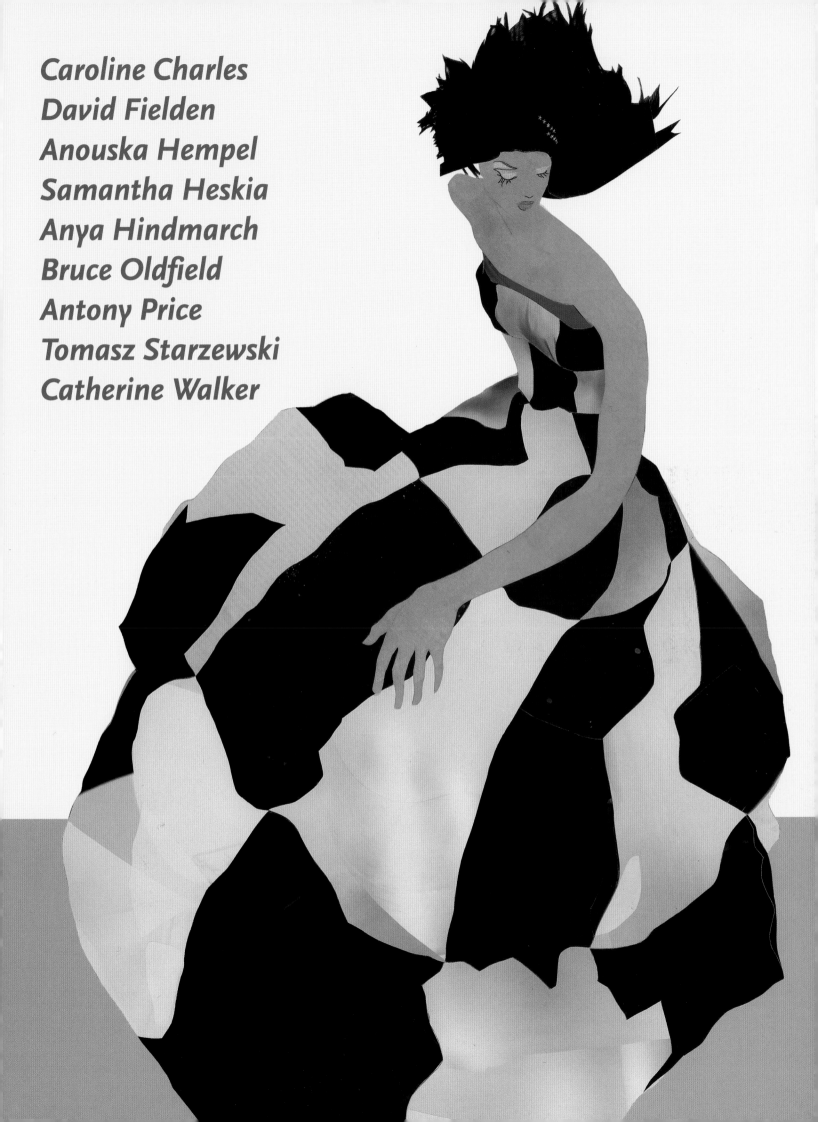

Caroline Charles
David Fielden
Anouska Hempel
Samantha Heskia
Anya Hindmarch
Bruce Oldfield
Antony Price
Tomasz Starzewski
Catherine Walker

# CAROLINE CHARLES

# DAVID FIELDEN

# SAMANTHA HESKIA

# BRUCE OLDFIELD

# TOMASZ STARZEWSKI

# CATHERINE WALKER

Peek into any wine bar in the Fulham Road and you'll still find it packed to the gills with Taras, Jemimas and Annabels – but take a closer look and you'll see that they are far more sophisticated than their predecessors a decade ago. Even the Sloaney types are a lot more on the ball these days, says Tomasz Starzewski. 'Their horizons are broader than they were in the eighties and their taste levels have improved. London is going through a cultural boom at the moment and it is changing people's perceptions of fashion.'

Starzewski has never claimed to be at the cutting edge but he makes sure that his work is constantly evolving to appeal to a younger and more sophisticated clientele each season. 'There has always been a market for beautifully made garments that are discreet and easy, that don't scream out their origins, but look beautifully fitted and express their quality through subtlety. Bearing all these things in mind, you must remember that if you don't move with the times you will die with your last customer.'

*LEFT TO RIGHT:*
*Catherine Walker: Brown pinstripe trompe-l'oeil coat dress.*

*Caroline Charles: White piqué cotton suit.*

*Bruce Oldfield: Beaded cream wool suit.*

*Samantha Heskia: Bag with transparent plastic beads; handle with flower clusters.*

*Tomasz Starzewski: Double-breasted beige suit with ivory-look beads on sleeve.*

*David Fielden: White crepe trouser suit with pixel print.*
Illustration Camilla Dixon.

## ANOUSKA HEMPEL

## ANYA HINDMARCH

## BRUCE OLDFIELD

## ANTONY PRICE

## CATHERINE WALKER

The Sloane Ranger is now designer clad rather than got up in the good old Pringle and pearls that Princess Di exported to the rest of the world. She has come of age and found her new figureheads in bleached blond 'It' girls like Tamara Beckwith and Caprice Bourret, and aristo-models like Stella Tennant and Honor Fraser.

As for designers, a whole new coterie of British couturiers are at her beck and call, creators of both smart daywear and ostentatious evening gowns. What is different, however, is that the tweedy suit and crinolined ballgown that we associate with this rarefied group of designers has been adapted to a clientele who will just as easily spend their inheritance at Prada and Gucci.

'You must constantly reassess where fashion is moving or you'll end up dead as a dodo,' says designer David Fielden, and he rejects the popular notion that eveningwear is centred round 'a kind of ghastly frivolity' by concentrating on a modern, streamlined silhouette that is as much about issuing a challenge to the wearer as about providing garments that are sexy and modern. For him and others of his kind, the late 1990s have witnessed a sea change in attitudes. Don't expect to see a dowager duchess dressed in Alexander McQueen, but do be prepared for a little less frou frou and much more fashion these days.

*LEFT TO RIGHT:*
*Bruce Oldfield: Copper, beaded, chiffon dress.*

*Anya Hindmarch: Black ostrich-feather bag.*

*Antony Price: Red and gold leather evening outfit with separate skirt in two panels; bodice over the top, laced at back.*

*Catherine Walker: Asymmetric dress in peach chiffon beaded all over in peach sequins and pearls, with rosettes.*

*Anouska Hempel: Black draped dress.*
Illustration Camilla Dixon.

OPPOSITE: *Interior of Vent, Ledbury Road.*

THIS PAGE: *Alan and Karen Beagle, in the Beagle Gallery, Westbourne Grove.* Photos David White.

# NOTTING HILL GATE

*'We all like Ledbury Road very much — the owner of Vent has a wonderful, funny habit of taking photographs of his customers'* – **CHRISTIAN LACROIX**

FOR LOCAL GIRL STELLA MCCARTNEY AND FOR INTERNATIONAL DESIGNERS SUCH AS DONNA KARAN, JEAN-PAUL GAULTIER AND MIUCCIA PRADA, NOTTING HILL GATE IS AN ALADDIN'S CAVE OF INSPIRATION. FREQUENT VISITOR CHRISTIAN LACROIX WRITES: NOTTING HILL GATE EPITOMIZES A CERTAIN LONDON SPIRIT DEAR TO OUR FRENCH MINDS AND DEAR TO PEOPLE OF MY GENERATION FOR WHOM MOVIES LIKE 'BLOW-UP' AND 'THE KNACK' OR TV SERIES LIKE 'THE AVENGERS' SYMBOLIZE ENGLAND FOR ALL TIME. THE POWER OF SUCH AN AREA IS THAT IT CONNECTS WITH THE MOODS OF THE PERIODS WE HAVE LIVED THROUGH BUT STILL REMAINS FAITHFUL TO A TIMELESS WORLD WHICH IS CALLED STYLE. WE ALL LIKE LEDBURY ROAD VERY MUCH — THE OWNER OF VENT HAS A WONDERFUL, FUNNY HABIT OF TAKING PHOTOGRAPHS OF HIS CUSTOMERS. HE SELLS

SEVENTIES CLOTHES, AMONG OTHER THINGS. I'M NOT SO FOND OF THE SEVENTIES MYSELF, BECAUSE I USED TO WEAR THOSE CLOTHES, BUT HIS ARE ESPECIALLY ATTRACTIVE.

I ALSO LIKE THE FACT THAT YOU CAN FIND IN NOTTING HILL NEW AND SPECIAL ITEMS SUCH AS LULU GUINNESS HANDBAGS WHICH MY WIFE IS CRAZY ABOUT • • • • • • •

**opposite, top left and centre left:** Orford & Swan, purveyor of couture textiles and accessories, The Pink Room, Kensington Church Street • • • • **opposite top centre:** Lulu Guinness handbags, Ledbury Road • • • • **opposite top right:** Bag by Bill Amberg (top) and jewelry by Solange Azagury-Partridge (bottom) • • • • **opposite bottom left:** Tom's Deli, Westbourne Grove • • • • • **opposite bottom centre:** Vent (proprietor: Simon Heah), Westbourne Grove • • • • • • **opposite bottom right:** The Cross, Portland Road

WHAT MAKES THE AREA FASHIONABLE IS ITS HIGH BOHEMIAN SPIRIT MIXED NOWADAYS WITH EVERYTHING WHICH DEFINES OUR OWN TIME: ETHNIC MIXTURES, FREEDOM OF

RELATIONSHIPS AND OPEN-MINDED COMMUNITIES. IT'S NOT THE SELF-ASSURANCE OF THE WEST END NOR THE FASHIONABLE 'BOURGEOISIE' OF CHELSEA, NOR THE TOUGH,

WORKING-CLASS FEELING OF BERMONDSEY. IT'S ALL THESE THINGS MIXED TOGETHER. NOT SO FAR FROM AIRY SUBURBS WITH QUIET STREETS, YET WITH AN AUTHENTIC

ATMOSPHERE — NOT TOO FASHIONABLE. IN THE MARKET THERE ARE GROCERY STORES MIXED WITH JEWELRY AND VINTAGE CLOTHES SHOPS. THE MIX IS IMPORTANT

BECAUSE IT MEANS THAT REAL PEOPLE LIVE THERE. I LIKE SOME OF THE TRENDY SHOPS UNDER THE BRIDGE: THEY ARE ALWAYS CHANGING — NEW DESIGNERS COME AND GO.

*AND I LIKE BEST OF ALL WHAT IS AT THE END — THE STRANGE, POOR, HUMBLE NOTHINGS, ALL THE THINGS THAT ARE PLACED FOR SALE RIGHT ON THE GROUND — THIS IS A*

*REAL TREASURE TROVE FOR ME* • • • • • • • • • • • • • • • • • • • • • • • • • • • • • • • • • • • • • • • • • • • • • • • • • • • • • • • • • • • • • • • • • • •

**opposite left:** Portobello Green, near Ladbroke Grove, where thrift-shop chic, bric-a-brac and doughnut stands jostle under plastic canopies • • • • • • • • • • • • •

• • • • • • • • • • • • • • • • • • • • • • • • • • • • • • • • •

**centre:** Clock above the flower stall, Westbourne Grove • • • • • • • • • • • • • • • • • • • • • • • • • • • • • • • • • • **right:** Portobello Green

THE MIX OF PERSONALITIES THAT YOU FIND IN ALL THE DIFFERENT SHOPS GIVES NOTTING HILL A UNIQUE APPEAL. EACH ONE EMPHASIZES THE NEIGHBOURHOOD'S CHARACTER. IT'S A LIGHT-HANDED SENSE OF STYLE AND FASHION, ALLOWING FOR VERY INDIVIDUAL CHOICE AND MAKING FOR A HIGHLY UNCONVENTIONAL COMMUNITY. DIFFERENCE, SELF-EXPRESSION AND AN UNCOMMON CREATIVITY PROVIDE THE CLUES TO THIS NEW FASHIONABLENESS. WHEN YOU ARE IN LOVE, AS I AM, WITH BRITAIN, LONDON AND NOTTING HILL GATE, IT DOES NOT MEAN THAT YOU ARE OBSESSSED WITH THE BANAL CLICHÉS OF TRADITIONAL LONDON, LIKE BLACK TAXIS AND VICTORIAN SHOPS, BUT RATHER WITH WHATEVER INSPIRED MIKE LEIGH, STEPHEN FREARS AND KEN LOACH — THAT'S THE TRUTH OF THE COUNTRY • • • • • • • • • • • • • • • • • • •

**opposite:** Portobello Road • • • • • • • **this page, top left:** Annette Olivieri, owner of Euphoria, Portobello Green Arcade • • •
• • • • **top centre:** Frank Akinsete, owner of Souled Out, in the Cobden Club • • • • • • • **top right:** The architect Yen Yen Teh in Space, Westbourne Grove (designed by
Yen Yen Teh and Tom Dixon) • • • • • • **above left:** Nick Hart in 192, Kensington Park Road • • • • • • • **above right:** Naz in The Merchant of Europe, Portobello Road

# HAUTE HIPPIE

Nigel Atkinson

Ally Capellino

Neisha Crosland

Helen David

Eley Kishimoto

Georgina von Etzdorf

Ghost

Elspeth Gibson

Abe Hamilton

Lainey Keogh

Stella McCartney

Rifat Ozbek

Zandra Rhodes

Clements Ribeiro

Wallace Sewell

THIS PAGE: Stella McCartney mint green silk slip dress with a lace slip on top.
Photo Rankin, 1996.

OPPOSITE: Ghost pink embroidered asymmetric dress, embroidered padded coat, leather neckpiece and cowboy boots, Autumn/Winter 1997–98.
Photo Ram & Fab.

# CLEMENTS RIBEIRO

'Clements Ribeiro makes graphic knits
and has a succulent sense of colour'

SUZY MENKES, FASHION WRITER, INTERNATIONAL HERALD TRIBUNE

'One for sorrow; two for joy.' In British fashion, the combined talents of Suzanne Clements and Inacio Ribeiro resemble the lucky pairing of magpies. They hunt for themes, they pillage archives, and through mixing old ideas in new combinations, they have won an international following.

Clements Ribeiro have gained inspiration for their collections from such diverse sources as Cuban costume, the bourgeois tastes of British suburbia and the snowy landscapes of C.S. Lewis's Narnia. They epitomize eclecticism, and despite the fact that Ribeiro is Brazilian, they are the first designers to key into the British notion of 'charity shop chic' through a style that fuses disparate stylistic elements into a coherent image. 'When I was growing up, we moved around the whole time,' says Clements, 'and you had to be able to assimilate fast because things were different wherever you ended up, whether it was the Home Counties or abroad. It makes designing far more exciting when you can draw on so many elements. It's not breaking the rules, but simply observing how they are interpreted around you.'

Their paths crossed at Central St Martins, where they graduated with first class honours in 1991. By 1992 they had married and a year later the label was born. 'The fact that Inacio is Brazilian and I'm from a very British background is very important to the end product,' says Clements. 'We fight all the time, and we may not even design the collection in the same country, which makes the phone bills astronomical – but the conflict of ideas always brings something exciting to each collection.'

In addition to combining fabrics and shapes, the pair also advocate adopting couture fabrics for basic daywear, cashmere for summer T-shirts and furnishing chintz for separates. In this way they gently subvert what the British deem to be appropriate attire. And the formula seems to be working. Their signature striped cashmere knits in offbeat colourways (launched as part of their womenswear collection for Spring/Summer 1996) were possibly one of the most copied garments of the decade.

But above all, Clements Ribeiro are superb decorative artists, employing every technique from crude embroidery inspired by Brazilian artist Bispo on large peasant skirts to tiny, floral appliqués in crystal on bias-cut crepe dresses. They also originated the craze for Mongolian lamb trims on jackets. 'Though everything in fashion today is a repeat on a cycle, the technology available to the designer is updated each season, so we can take accepted wisdom and reinvent it,' says Clements.

Perhaps Clements Ribeiro symbolize what contemporary British, or – more specifically – London fashion is: the numerous cross-cultural references, the mixing of shabby and chic, and the diversity of influence, all of which reflect the mixtures in London society. And with a growing international following, they're exporting their talents to the rest of the world. 'What makes me happiest is the thought that people around the world actually save up their money so that they can buy our clothes,' says Clements. 'It's really humbling, but exciting at the same time.'

TOP LEFT: Clothes by Clements Ribeiro, on display in the window of Liberty, Regent Street, W1. Photo Dee Jay, 1996.

ABOVE AND LEFT: Designs from the 'Atlantis etc.' collection of Spring/Summer 1998. Photo Dee Jay.

OPPOSITE: The Spring/Summer 1997 collection. Photo Dee Jay.

# ZANDRA RHODES

Textile artist and dress designer Zandra Rhodes is the high priestess of the haute hippie genre. Since her graduation from the Royal College of Art in the late 1960s, she has been turning women into contemporary Titanias by cutting prints so that the logic and placement of the design define the garment.

In a field where novelty is prized, Rhodes's work over the years has been remarkable both for its consistency and for its refusal to kowtow to the whims and vagaries of fashion trends. 'I've been working with ideas on how print works on the body since the 1960s,' she says. 'I can't and won't design for people who hide in a corner. Fashion should be about becoming a peacock.'

Because her clothes are fanciful and fantastical, using volume to display her prints to best advantage, they do not date. Her references are timeless, from the fragile pink chiffon of the dress worn by the late Princess of Wales, with a hem like a curtain of melting icicles, to the vibrantly printed, full pleated skirts and long, gathered sleeves inspired by Ukranian festival dress.

First and foremost, however, Rhodes is a textile designer: the imagery in each collection relates in a quixotic way to various journeys she has made and cultures she has witnessed. 'My approach is multicultural,' she says. 'It started with very local, tangible impressions – the supermarket, TV shows and the Blackpool illuminations – and later, as the pattern of my life became more international, the influences in my designs expanded to take in foreign cultures.' These show in the Native American feather motifs which inspired her collections in the early 1970s, as well as in later images of Aztec Temples, the Peking Opera and Masai tribespeople.

Her techniques are self-taught: garments do not conform to the strictures of traditional dressmaking, they work with her prints, not against them, and are often cut flat or with minimal shaping to display the designs. This is apparent both in the pared-back beauty of her 'butterfly' dresses and in the mad cacophony of embroidery and slashing of her seminal punk collection.

Rhodes has a successful business in the USA, where she remains one of the UK's best known designers, and as fashion steers itself away from the minimalism of the mid-1990s, she is poised to influence a whole new generation of peacocks.

'I can't and won't design for people who hide in a corner. Fashion should be about becoming a peacock'

OPPOSITE: *Zandra Rhodes in her studio, 1997.* Photo Bernhardt von Spreckelsen.

# MATTHEW WILLIAMSON

'I want to create clothes that show their craft

and look special and individual'

In his first catwalk show in September 1997, Matthew Williamson put colour back into fashion with a capsule collection of eleven stunning outfits, entitled 'Electric Angels'. In the audience sunglasses were donned as combinations of shocking pink, tangerine, turquoise and lemon combined with black to form a liquorice-allsorts collection of E-number brights.

Every piece was handcrafted: 'I want to create clothes that show their craft, and that look special and individual,' Williamson says. His showroom is bedecked with bright plastic flowers and trinkets brought back from frequent trips to India where the more intricate pieces of his work are embroidered and beaded. For not only are his clothes bright, they are also delicate, and involve painstaking work – an embroidered peacock feather with a beaded eye on a chiffon dress, for example, or a tiny cashmere cardigan stitched with butterflies. His fragile beaded handbags – first spotted on the arms of numerous supermodels – are like ethereal lobster nets and his simple silk tops with lace edging combine electrifying mixes of hot colour.

'I love using colour, but I also like the way people mix garments,' Williamson says. 'Even the way I design is eclectic – by putting unusual colours together and making use of many different handcrafted techniques, so that things don't look as if they've come off a massive production line. I want to develop the business slowly so that it keeps that special feeling of handcraftedness.'

# RIFAT OZBEK

'Doing a collection is like composing a story or a play. It should take the wearer on a journey, introduce him or her to new horizons and give them the courage to experiment'

Rifat Ozbek's collections are the Baedeker of the fashion world. Although he may have chosen to make London his home after coming to the UK from his native Turkey to study architecture, he creates collections that are a pastiche of ethnicity, plundering cultural references worldwide. 'There's a beauty born out of necessity in a lot of foreign cultures,' he says. 'People wear what they've got, because fashion is a luxury they can't afford. When you see a woman wearing a man's knitted waistcoat and a brightly printed dirndl skirt, it's a combination we wouldn't dream of in the West, yet it can be transformed into clothing we understand.'

As fashion anthropologist, Ozbek has a take on ethnicity that is more sophisticated than simple reinterpretation. In his Indonesian collection (Spring/Summer 1993), traditional sarongs were mixed with strict military tailoring, so combining the native cultures of the Islands with the uniforms of Dutch colonials. Other collections have used Native American embroidery and beading on traditional Confederate military uniforms, or have taken their direction from such diverse stimuli as fencing jackets, Central European gypsies and the Haiti of dictator Papa Doc. 'My methods of research are very simple,' says Ozbek. 'When I find a culture that inspires me I immerse myself in it completely, but I never revisit a source of inspiration. If something is worthwhile it will stick

in my mind, and I'll act on it – you should never have to look at the same thing twice.'

Colour and print are also essential in making the ethnic urbane. A simple linen shirt is decorated with Moroccan embroidery; a hooded bodysuit in microfibre has distorted patterns inspired by Moorish tiles; a polar fleece top has Romany florals burnt out of the fabric. 'Doing a collection is like composing a story or a play. It should take the wearer on a journey, introduce him or her to new horizons and give them the courage to experiment,' says Ozbek. And, he adds, 'It should be sexy.'

Perhaps Ozbek's best remembered collection is his least typical. While the fashion world was in the last throes of Power Dressing, his 'New Age' show for Spring/Summer 1990 moved away from the vibrant mixes of ethnic cultures that personify his name, towards a collection of all white that symbolized purity, strength and spirituality.

From ethnic to barely there, it seems there is nothing that Ozbek won't turn his hand to, 'Except you'll never see underwear with my name woven into the elastic.' Nor will you find minimal black suits and conservative two-pieces: 'Other designers can get on with dull colours and minimalism. Clashing colours and cultures can sometimes look vulgar, but they're more inspirational than a two-piece and definitely more inspiring to design.'

OPPOSITE: *Yellow rayon snake-embossed tunic, Future Ozbek, Autumn/Winter 1996–97.*
Photo Ram & Fab.

BELOW LEFT: *Autumn/Winter 1994–95.*
Photo Chris Moore.

BELOW CENTRE: *Future Ozbek, Autumn/Winter 1996–97.*
Photo Ram & Fab.

BELOW RIGHT: *Spring/Summer 1996.*
Photo Chris Moore.

# LAINEY KEOGH

'Lainey Keogh's seaweed beds of knitting are works of art'

SUZY MENKES, FASHION WRITER, INTERNATIONAL HERALD TRIBUNE

LEFT TOP: *Constance, wearing the 'Fish Bathing Dress', in woven fabric with a fine gauze knit lining and beaded straps. Spring/Summer 1998.* Photo Tim Griffiths.

LEFT CENTRE: *Jodie Kidd, wearing the 'Long Gold River Dress', in all-gold woven fabric, with gold gauze knit underlining. The fabric has pearls woven into it. Spring/Summer 1998.* Photo Tim Griffiths.

LEFT BOTTOM: *Kate Moss, wearing the 'Silver River Dress', a slip dress, the top of which has crochet motifs joined together. The bottom of the dress is of silver woven fabric with fringing. Spring/Summer 1998.* Photo Tim Griffiths.

RIGHT: *Marianne Faithful, wearing a fine-knit shirt dress over a latex corset. The dress is made from fine, shiny, semi-metallic yarns. Spring/Summer 1998.* Photo Tim Griffiths.

OPPOSITE: *Sophie Dahl, wearing a purple latex corset which laces up the back. Over it is a 'Lavender Breeze Air Coat' woven from fine embroidery threads. Spring/Summer 1998.* Photo Tim Griffiths.

Since the late 1980s Lainey Keogh has been one of Ireland's foremost designers, with a growing band of customers who understand that her tactile creations have little to do with anything conventional knitwear has seen before. For all her pieces – whether knitted, crocheted or woven by hand – have an appeal that is as strong in the minimalist setting of Barney's New York as it is in the Kilkenny Design shop in Dublin's city centre. Homespun – maybe. Quaint – never.

When much of Ireland's domestic talent has failed to shrug off the folksy image that does little more than gladden the hearts of American tourists, Keogh is unique in that her designs make women feel sexy and voluptuous. Hugging a woman wearing Lainey Keogh is to revel in what she calls the 'touch factor'– the capacity of each piece to both comfort and arouse. Confronted with a rail of her garments, one might easily imagine that her fairytale creations in boggy colours, deep luxurious piles and amorphous shapes are the product of a highly eccentric mind. Not so. Keogh's mantra of colour, texture and fit singles her out as a designer who knows exactly what her customer wants. 'When you go into a shop, there are three things which strike you immediately: the colour, the shape and how the garment feels against the skin,' she says. 'It has to feel fantastic.'

Yarn to Keogh is what tweed is to Westwood or jersey to Jean Muir – the root of her creative power and an obsession which has spawned such diverse materials as knitted steel, giant loopy mohair coats (knitted on jumbo 12-inch needles) and gold filigree twisted into glittering crochet yarn. 'Once when I was researching an autumn collection,' she says, 'I visited all the major furriers in London just to feel the pelts. They're so sexy, with a kind of raw energy that brings out the hunter in man, and makes them objects of desire on the backs of women.' The upshot? – a wide range of brushed wools that resembled animal skin, yet involved no cruelty, only phenomenal sales.

# ABE HAMILTON

## 'I don't even want people to think of my clothes as fashion'

Look inside the neck of an Abe Hamilton garment and you'll find a label on which three etiolated daisies dance above a delicate, scratchy signature. But you don't need to be a handwriting expert to detect that Hamilton's signature exemplifies the fragility and gentleness of his designs. 'I don't even want people to think of my clothes as fashion, more as something that has always existed,' he says.

The innate romanticism of Hamilton's designs is what makes his clothes so popular, especially with those women who reject the blatant luxury of so many designer labels. Even the normally brassy Madonna took on a demure aspect in one of his signature lace dresses. Yet Hamilton's clothes are less about frills and escapism than about an earthy simplicity that celebrates women rather than turning them into dolls or fashion victims. 'I have a customer who bought the same dress as Madonna. She must be in her mid-forties and is very curvy. She looks fantastic in the dress because she has the confidence to show off her body, which makes her sexy in a very natural, uncontrived way.'

From his beginnings as a chef, to his work as an artist and subsequently designer, Hamilton has etched his sensuality into his creations. Fragile lace or delicate, featherweight silks in sunbleached pastels are cut into simple, almost deconstructed, silhouettes which caress rather than constrain the form and are feminine without being a travesty. His colour sense is naturalistic and delicate – a Hamilton dress may be a rich tangerine or a delicate blue, but it is never anything too razzle dazzle or showbiz, despite his following of starlets and It Girls. Like Hamilton himself – a tall, gaunt figure, with deep-set eyes and slender fingers – his clothes are saved from being too fairytale by their lack of pretension and their spare beauty. He is neither precious nor prone to the affectation so prevalent in the world of fashion. He's just an ordinary bloke, designing surprisingly gentle clothes.

*ABOVE: Preparing for the Spring/Summer 1998 show.* Photo Thierry Chomel.

*RIGHT: Models applaud after the Spring/Summer 1998 show.* Photo Thierry Chomel.

'All women designers understand that you
have to design with real people in mind'

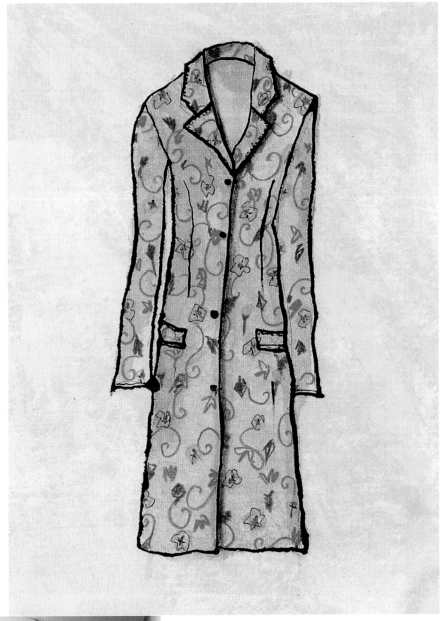

Beneath Elspeth Gibson's gentle demeanour is a designer with a firm grip on what the modern woman really wants: clothes with a certain romance but which reflect today's need for realism.

She has the knack of creating feminine clothes which escape being prissy or twee. She can make you look fragile and beautiful, but it's never the stuff of fairytale. She is bold in a gentle way, and her clever manipulation of fabrics and silhouettes produces sexy, womanly clothes. She is happier to have her customer mooch about in trainers than in stilettos, and prefers her designs to be mixed with second-hand clothes than worn from head to toe. 'I love seeing people in my things who don't look too contrived. A simple lace skirt is far more exciting when you combine it with unexpected elements.'

She uses an eclectic mix of fabrics, including lace, silk, satin, crepe, embroidered georgette and a rabbit's foot velvet that has a pile reminiscent of that ghoulish good luck symbol. Her shapes are simple, focusing on luxury rather than ostentation. 'I hate that "everything-but-the-kitchen-sink" ritziness you find in so much eveningwear. For me the silhouette has to be simple and the fabric luxurious, even if it's a basic cotton for a little summer dress.'

Her charming, strappy dresses have made their mark on the British consciousness through a combination of simple lines and delicate embellishment in the form of oxidized sequins and fragile bugle beads. 'Proportion is just as important as decoration and they must go hand in hand if a garment is to be successful. Although I love using unusual and beautiful fabrics, if the line of the shoulder is not cut properly it can make the difference between a neck that looks like a swan, or one that resembles a joint of meat. It's that important,' she states.

Gibson's idols are of her own generation: young women who are confident in their femininity, who seek a certain romanticism that is relevant to their daily lives. 'I don't deny that I design romantic clothes, but they're not meant for an idyll. My customer wants to wear her beaded dress while dodging traffic in Oxford Street, not while sitting on a swing in an orchard.'

# STELLA McCARTNEY

'I don't want to change my background, but I do want people to judge what I design for its own sake'

If her surname were Bloggs, the story might have taken a different turn, but when your father is Sir Paul McCartney, you come to regard the media spotlight as a necessary peril of famous parentage.

However, let us imagine for a moment that she is anyone from anytown UK, and examine what she does rather than who she is. For Stella McCartney, chief designer at Chloé, is very much a product of her environment, in that her designs reflect the diversity of London in a way that encapsulates the bustle of Portobello Market, the café society of Soho, and a crowd of beautiful young things who are happy to mix vintage and thrift-store clothing with the odd designer purchase. 'I'm obsessed,' she laughs. 'I could spend days picking through things in antique markets looking for the right piece of lace for a trim, or a brilliant button for a jacket. There's a quality that you don't find in modern clothing – the finish, the way the tailors didn't cut corners when they constructed a jacket, and a real feeling of craftsmanship.'

Like Galliano and Westwood before her, McCartney relies heavily on modernizing historically inspired shapes for the late-1990s customer. But her designs are younger and more upbeat than those of the other Brits showing in Paris – closer to a Saturday night on the town than to the costume exhibits at the V&A. For McCartney, the antique elements in her clothing are subtle rather than all-defining. During her time as a student at St Martins, she worked part-time for the Savile Row tailor Edward Sexton, who served as a consultant on the Chloé show 'to help us get it right, as Chloé doesn't have experience of making that kind of tailoring in house'.

Her preoccupation with the antique surfaced once again in her debut at Chloé in October 1997 – a show which mixed vintage elements such as Belle Epoque boned corsetry with simple, nifty silk camisoles in shocking pink, trimmed with ribbons of black lace. McCartney says of this collection, 'I didn't design it with a theme in mind; it's about my friends, and what I get up to when I'm in London. I'm not trying to shock people.' The show featured rich fabrics in dusty pastels cut into soft shapes. Some pieces were ruched, some plain, some ornamented with witty embroideries, others sparkling with diamanté. Some were young and gamine, others were more ladylike: 'Before Chloé, when I was doing my own collection, everyone wore my clothes, from my mum and her friends to girls my own age.

If they can all find things that they like, I must be getting the balance right,' she says.

The formula seems to have worked. After the well-received 1997 show, where Sir Paul and his wife, Linda, were happy to play second fiddle to their daughter's designs, Chloé became more than just an also-ran in the French fashion stakes for the first time since the mid-seventies. Founded in 1952, the company had gained its reputation with expensive, romantic clothes with a louche, bohemian appeal but had lost its signature after successive design appointments muddled its message. By the mid-nineties, its prestige had slipped into the second division of Parisian fashion houses. The appointment in 1996 of McCartney – then a recent graduate with only two collections under her belt – to replace Karl Lagerfeld sent shockwaves through the fashion industry, but in fact Chloé got just what it desperately needed – a young designer with a young outlook.

Being a McCartney and not a Bloggs may have had a lot to do with shaping her career, but it also makes her the target of particularly stringent criticism. 'I don't want to change my background,' she says, 'but I do want people to judge what I design for its own sake – that's not too much to ask, is it?'

OPPOSITE: Cali Rand in silk and lace slip dress and vintage veil for Autumn/Winter 1997, photographed in Stella McCartney's studio in Notting Hill Gate, September 1996. Photo Mary McCartney.

ABOVE: Silver mesh metal top with silver thread straps, worn with tailored trousers in birdseye fabric, September 1996.

LEFT: Kate Moss modelling Stella McCartney's pale blue silk swallow print scarf dress at the designer's first collection for Chloé (Spring/Summer 1998), held at the Paris Opéra, October 1997.

Photos Mary McCartney.

# ALLY CAPELLINO

## 'I'm fascinated by fabric, the way it can be architectural'

Since 1979, Alison Lloyd – the creative force behind Ally Capellino – has become used to being mistaken for her brandname. 'Some people even think I'm a man,' she says ruefully. What she omits to mention, however, is that the name, chosen for its decorative squiggle, has not only become synonymous with the diminutive woman who creates the collection, but is one of Britain's best-loved design labels.

Started primarily as an accessories label ('capellino' means 'little hat'), Ally Capellino swiftly transformed itself into one of the important brands of the mid-1980s by reinventing traditional English clothing in a quirky, upbeat way. 'We were messing around with tweeds and other traditional fabrics and were updating styles from the forties and fifties before this became really high-street,' says Lloyd. Next came linens and a naturalistic approach to fashion. Subsequently, Ally Capellino has become a designer label which, though it does not pretend to be cutting edge, nevertheless successfully translates modern ideas into wearable clothes. 'It's about classic ideas with a challenge,' says Lloyd.

A typical Ally Capellino garment is hard to define. It may take the form of a simple, bias-cut T-shirt in supersoft microfibre, easy to design yet covetable in its execution. Or it may be a boiled-wool felt coat with matching cape that has an ovoid shape and a colour like the scarlet of a cardinal's robe. 'I'm fascinated by fabric, the way it can be architectural. When a building is constructed, the fabric is all-defining; it's the same with fashion: you can be experimental in a constructive way, and not just for kicks.'

For Lloyd, the role of designer is linked to more than fashion. Though she may choose to show during London Fashion Week, she is equally happy at occasions like the launch of her 'ao' diffusion collection at London's Serpentine Gallery (where she sponsored a show by New York artist Jean-Michel Basquiat). Her preference is for low-key, thought-provoking presentations, where robotic models enter from all directions wearing her deceptively simple designs. Since the 1980s Ally Capellino has transformed itself into an experimental design house with an enlightened customer who approves its mantra that clothes need to be both wearable and quietly avant-garde.

*ABOVE LEFT: Alison Lloyd, designer of Ally Capellino, at the end of the Spring/Summer 1998 catwalk show.*
Photo Tim Griffiths.

*LEFT: Models at the Spring/Summer 1998 show.*
Photo Tim Griffiths.

*BELOW: Autumn/Winter 1996–97.*
Photo Dee Jay.

*OPPOSITE: A page from the Ally Capellino design books for Spring/Summer 1997.*
Courtesy Ally Capellino.

*OPPOSITE, INSET: Design for Spring/Summer 1998.*
Photo Tim Griffiths.

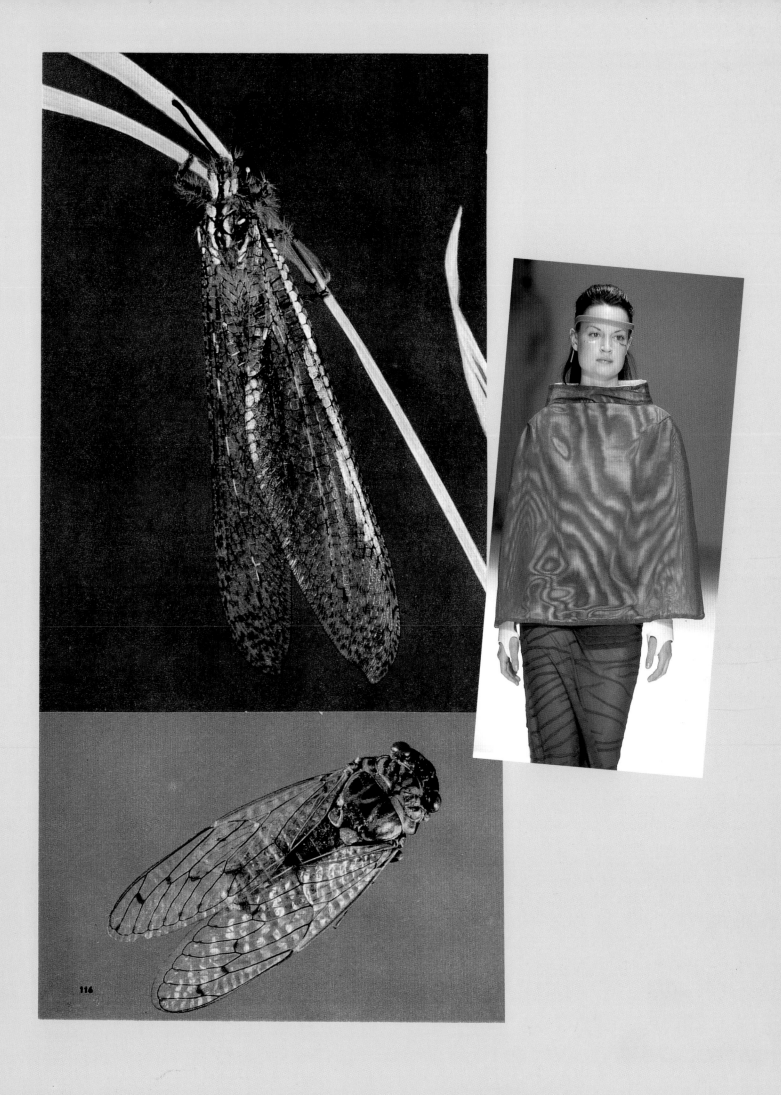

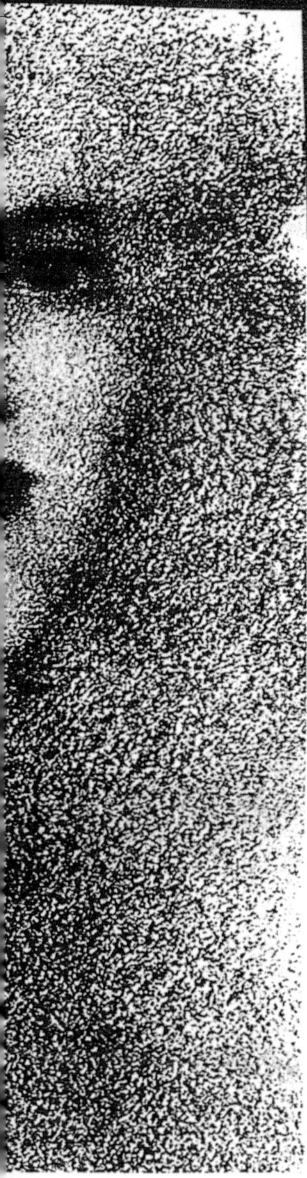

Pretty, coloured
embroideries
lace - like

# GHOST

## 'We design affordable clothes for real women'

Tanya Sarne is cool. With her flurry of curly hair and scarlet-heeled Christian Louboutin boots, she exudes a manic energy that inspires her hip, young workforce to reinvent the wheel each season. The fluid viscose pieces that she creates owe their success both to the ease and comfort they give the wearer and to a kind of mystique which keeps them at the forefront of fashion. Fashion editors wear them, as do supermodels, who are only too happy to take payment of a few Ghost dresses in return for appearing in the runway show. Even women of a certain age who would feel uncomfortable in other designer clothes love the Ghost look because it is so forgiving. And because Sarne's mantra is 'real clothes for real women', Ghost garments are not only sexy, they are also crease resistant and machine washable.

When she founded the label in 1984 (the name derives from a friend's warning: 'You don't have a ghost of a chance'), Sarne decided to explore the concept of 'designing affordable clothes for real women – clothes that allowed them to look different', and, like the alchemist discovering the philosopher's stone, she happened to chance on a type of viscose that could be shrunken and dyed to create a fabric with the consistency of vintage crepe, which absorbed colour, and which skimmed the curves of the body without clinging like a limpet. 'The idea was around already, but it was so complicated to get right; you had to be a masochist to try,' says Sarne. The untreated viscose has a quality not unlike surgical gauze, yet its finished sister, which shrinks by 40 percent in the finishing process, has the texture of soft parchment.

Ghost's designs may save a fortune in dry-cleaning bills, but this is not enough. The collection must evolve each season to retain its individuality. Clingy in the eighties, soft and flowing in the nineties, it is never frumpy or boring despite its easy-to-wear appeal. And though numerous copyists are always snapping at Sarne's heels, her designs retain an edge both in quality and in their ability to set new trends at an extraordinary rate. 'Some designer clothes are like straitjackets; you can't run for a bus in them, or feel confident that they don't make your bum look huge. That is the antithesis of what we aim to create,' says Sarne, 'but all the same we try to move things on every season by offering our customer both the well-loved classics and other pieces that challenge them to be brave.'

*ABOVE: Models backstage at the Spring/Summer 1998 collection.* Photo Gavin Bond.

*LEFT AND OPPOSITE: Two pages from the Ghost design books for Spring/Summer 1998. This is described as 'a haunted collection, inspired by spirits and the intangible beauty of nature'.* Illustrations Susanne Deeken.

# NIGEL ATKINSON   NEISHA CROSLAND
# HELEN DAVID   ELEY KISHIMOTO
# GEORGINA VON ETZDORF   WALLACE SEWELL

In the context of fashion, textile designers are often overlooked, or at best considered 'arty types' with a propensity for the purely decorative. But for designer Neisha Crosland, the way an image is repeated on a textile is as fundamental to the rhythm of a good design as a beat is to music. For Helen David of English Eccentrics, colour sense is equated with perfect pitch. Weavers Harriet Wallace-Jones and Emma Sewell of Wallace Sewell painstakingly hand-dye the blends of yarn that make up their woven scarves and throws in a decrepit washing machine in the corner of their studio.

'There are so many preconceptions about textiles designers that are rubbish,' says Georgina von Etzdorf. 'Our work is linked to craftsmanship, our sense of colour is acute, and I can get inspiration from the carpet in the doctor's waiting room more readily than on some kind of clichéd exotic jaunt. What I design is decorative, but it's about subtlety and colour, and concerns clothing as much as accessories.'

If perception is half the battle, technique is of equal importance. For design duo Mark Eley and Wakako Kishimoto, their south London studio is home to any number of nauseous and noxious chemicals employed in manipulating materials in a way which pushes back the boundaries of printed textiles. Lying in a cardboard box are samples of scorched animal pelts for Alexander McQueen (Spring/Summer 1997), sugar paper foliage bonded onto wool for Sonja Nuttall (Autumn/Winter 1995) and handpainted roses on fragile devoré viscose from their own collection – not a typical textile studio

output. 'We don't see ourselves as textile designers, but as designers. It's about making marks directly onto the fabric, not sitting in a studio with a paintbrush,' says Kishimoto.

While Eley Kishimoto may dazzle with science, on the other side of town Nigel Atkinson has evolved a subtler technique which endows even the humblest fabrics and brocades with an embossed finish through their use of heat-reactive inks. 'I wanted to create fabrics with all the excitement of embroidered fabrics and brocades, yet without the labour,' he explains. For Atkinson, the term 'techno textiles', which is applied to so many contemporary textile designers, is inappropriate. He embraces the modern yet has a desire to confuse the bystander into believing that technologically produced textiles could be family heirlooms.

Above all, their understanding of and affiliation with fashion is pivotal to the work of these designers. A Helen David devoré scarf may festoon the neck of a wealthy theatregoer, but her work in fact goes beyond the confines of accessories. 'It's an easy assumption to make that textile designers are just good for a few scarves,' says David, summing up the quandary many find themselves in. 'Fashion print works in the context of how print moves on the body; you can't just work on a flat sheet of paper and foresee the end results without allying it to fashion. That's the secret.'

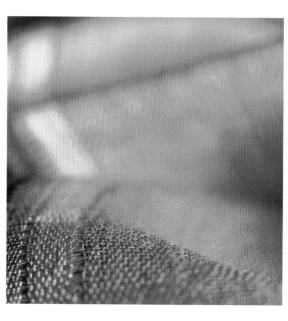

ABOVE: *Eley Kishimoto, 'Lingerie', Spring/Summer 1997.*

FAR LEFT: *Nigel Atkinson, multi-fluted wrap in red organza, 1997.*

LEFT: *Wallace Sewell, 'Rose no. 2', 1997.*

Photos Fleur Olby.

ABOVE: Helen David, English Eccentrics, 'Chrysanthemum', devoré satin, Spring/Summer 1998.

RIGHT: Georgina von Etzdorf, 'Lupin', silver/blue hand-beaded and embroidered metallic silk organza stole, Autumn/Winter 1997–98.

BELOW: Neisha Crosland, 'Sunburst', 1997.

Photos Fleur Olby.

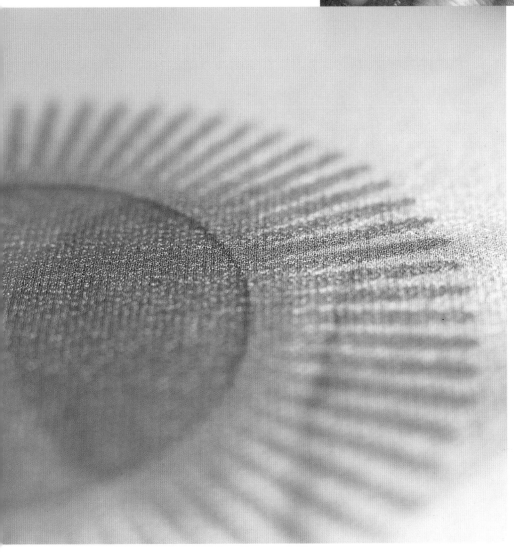

EAST
END

'I WANTED TO MOVE TO AN AREA WHERE I COULD WALK DOWN THE STREET AND BE COMPLETELY ANONYMOUS,' SAYS KATY ENGLAND, CREATIVE DIRECTOR AND MUSE TO BOTH

ALEXANDER MCQUEEN AND THE PARISIAN HOUSE OF GIVENCHY • • • • • • • • HER DECISION TO RELOCATE IN 1996 FROM THE DESPERATELY TRENDY LOCALE OF PORTOBELLO,

WHERE EVERY FELLOW-SHOPPER SEEMED TO BE A STYLIST OR MODEL, TO THE ROUGH-AND-READY AESTHETICS OF OLD STREET IN THE EAST OF LONDON IS ONE THAT SHE HAS

SELDOM REGRETTED • • • • • • • • 'IT'S SO MUCH MORE RELAXED HERE, NO ONE'S OBSESSIVELY TRYING TO BE FASHIONABLE THE WHOLE TIME, IT'S JUST A MIX OF REAL PEOPLE

GETTING ON WITH THEIR LIVES.' ALTHOUGH SHE'LL ADMIT THAT THE AREA'S ARCHITECTURE ISN'T UP TO MUCH, AND A FEW MORE TREES THAT WEREN'T GRIMY WITH

*'You have to mention The Bean, a coffee shop on the corner of Curtain Road and Rivington Street, because I drop in every morning for my caffeine fix – it's one of the most important places in my life – just perfect.'* KATY ENGLAND, CREATIVE DIRECTOR, ALEXANDER MCQUEEN

*POLLUTION WOULD MAKE A NICE ADDITION, THE NON-CONTRIVED ATMOSPHERE AND MIX OF SOCIAL AND ETHNIC CULTURES MORE THAN MAKE UP FOR A SHORTAGE OF GREENERY IN THE NEIGHBOURHOOD* • • • • • • • • • • • • • • • • • • • • • • • • • • • • • • • • • **opposite:** Katy England, Old Street • • • • • • • • • • • • • • • **top left:** Manhole cover, Brick Lane • • • • • • • • • • • • • • • • **top right:** The aptly named Fashion Street **above left:** Men's and women's shirts for Spring/Summer 1998 in Justin Oh's studio in Clerkenwell Green • • • • • • • • • • • • • • • • • **above right:** Graffiti in Boot Street • • • • • • • • • • • • • • • • • • • • • • • • • • • • • • • • • • • • • • • • • • • • • • • • • • • • • • • • • • • • • • • • • •

'YOU CAN SPEND YOUR TIME HERE HOW YOU WANT, WITHOUT THRONGS OF TOURISTS GIVING YOU THE ONCE OVER,' SAYS ENGLAND. 'SOMETIMES I WANDER DOWN TO BRICK LANE FOR A CURRY, OR VISIT THE FLEA MARKET THERE ON A SUNDAY MORNING AND CONTINUE ON FOR BREAKFAST AT COLUMBIA ROAD MARKET, WHERE YOU CAN WATCH PEOPLE FIGHTING OVER THE CHEAPEST TRAY OF GERANIUMS.' THE AREA IS NOW EQUALLY BUSY AFTER DARK, AS A SUCCESSION OF RESTAURANTS HAVE COLONIZED AN AREA WHICH WAS ONCE DEVOID OF LIFE AT SUNDOWN. IN ADDITION TO THE LEGENDARY CURRY HOUSES OF BRICK LANE, THE EAST END GOURMAND CAN SAMPLE TRADITIONAL ENGLISH FARE AT THE QUALITY CHOP HOUSE OR PACIFIC RIM CUISINE AT CICADA, AND THEN CATCH A LATE NIGHT FILM AT THE LUX CINEMA ON HOXTON SQUARE, OR WORK

LUX CINEMA

I PIECE
CHICKEN +
CHIPS + DINK
t 1 · 4o P

OFF THE CALORIES BY THRASHING AROUND TO THE LATEST TREND IN JUNGLE MUSIC AT THE NEIGHBOURING BLUE NOTE CLUB • • • • • • • • • • • • • • • •

**opposite top left:** The Bricklayer's Arms, Charlotte Road • • • • **opposite top right:** Tile from the interior of the Jerusalem Tavern, Britton Street • • • • **opposite bottom left:** Pellicci's, Bethnal Green Road • • • • **opposite bottom right:** A selection of condiments at the Quality Chop House, Farringdon Road • • • • • • • • • • • • • • **this page top left:** The Eagle, the pub mentioned in the famous rhyme 'Up and down the City Road, in and out the Eagle' – a favourite hangout of journalists • • • • **top right:** The Lux Cinema, Hoxton Square • • • • **above left:** Notice on the window of a kebab shop in Brick Lane • • • • **above right:** Queueing to get into the fashionable Blue Note club, Hoxton Square

*'Around here there are artists and craftspeople who are actually getting their hands dirty.'* KATY ENGLAND

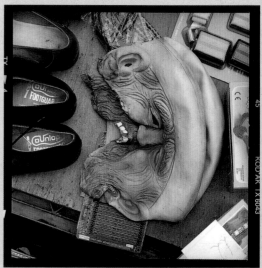

BUT FOR ALL EAST END DEVOTEES, THE SECRET OF THE AREA'S CHARM IS IN ITS INCONGRUITY. FROM HANDMADE LACQUER BOWLS AT THE NON-PROFIT-MAKING TRADE AND CARE STUDIO IN BUTTESLAND STREET, TO THE ELVIS MEMORABILIA SHOP, 'ELVISLY YOURS', ON SHOREDITCH HIGH STREET ('I'D MUCH RATHER WALK PAST SOMETHING LIKE THAT ON MY WAY TO WORK, THAN ANOTHER TWEE INTERIORS SHOP,' SAYS ENGLAND), THE EAST END THROWS UP SURPRISES WHICH EXIST FOR THE LOCALS RATHER THAN FOR VISITING VOYEURS. 'ONE OF MY FAVOURITES IS THE TATTOOIST "INTO YOU" ON ST JOHN'S STREET,' SAYS ENGLAND, WHO, TOGETHER WITH HER BOYFRIEND AND BEST FRIEND, OPTED FOR A BLACK PANTHER ON HER ARM. 'IT'S BRILLIANT BECAUSE THEY TAKE REAL CARE OVER THE DESIGN AND YOU HAVE TO BOOK A MONTH IN ADVANCE. IT'S

**opposite, top row, left to right:** The tattooist Curly at Into You, St John Street; Trade and Care, lacquer and ceramics studio, Buttesland Street; Relaxing at The Bean coffee

shop, Curtain Road • • • • • • • • • • **centre row, left to right:** Elvisly Yours, purveyor of Elvis memorabilia, Shoreditch High Street; Atlantis art supply store (where Hussein

Chalayan held his Spring/Summer 1998 and Autumn/Winter 1998–99 shows), Brick Lane; R. Aaronson Veneers, Redchurch Street • • • • • • • • • • **bottom row, left to right:**

Practising at Circus Space, Coronet Street; carriage wheels for sale at Columbia Road Market; stall, Club Row Market • • • • • • • • • • **above:** Eyes for sale, Club Row Market

# THE NEW GENERATION

CX
2.01

C203
STUDIO

C201      DYE ROOM

A201
STUDIO

Every year a hopeful group of candidates present themselves for interview for the MA course at Central Saint Martins. One by one, each potential McQueen enters the inner sanctum of course leader Louise Wilson, only to re-emerge, twenty minutes later, looking like someone who has just undergone root-canal treatment. For, once inside, candidates have to prove themselves worthy of a place on one of the top two fashion MA courses in the country.

Across town, in the more rarefied atmosphere of Kensington, Wendy Dagworthy is vetting students at the Royal College of Art, where she looks for candidates who will 'dictate to the industry and not be dictated to'. Both women are in the unenviable position of selecting the next graduate superstar to keep the torch of British fashion aflame. Yet, according to both, the Gallianos and Berardis are just a fraction of those who go on to pursue successful careers well out of the limelight. When asked what the mysterious ingredient is that makes Saint Martins and the Royal College of Art produce celebrities in such numbers, Wilson and Dagworthy offer different, but not contradictory answers.

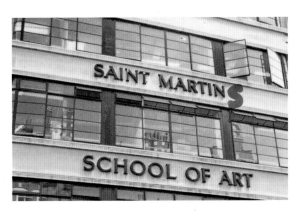

LEFT: *Howard Tangye's Fashion Drawing class, Saint Martins College of Art and Design. Tangye is at the back of the room, in the corner, wearing a beret. He taught both Julie Verhoeven and Camilla Dixon, whose work appears on pages 124–125 and 134–139.* Photo Tim Griffiths, 1998.

RIGHT: *Student cutting a pattern, Royal College of Art.* Photo © Royal College of Art.

RIGHT, SECOND FROM TOP: *St Martins, Long Acre building.* Photo Tim Griffiths, 1997.

RIGHT, SECOND FROM BOTTOM: *Shokooh Hakimi (right), pattern cutting tutor at St Martins, with a student.* Photo Tim Griffiths, 1998.

RIGHT, BOTTOM: *St Martins noticeboard with clippings on the work of former students.* Photo Tim Griffiths, 1998.

'London has always had the knack of producing talent,' says Dagworthy, who was herself a successful designer in the 1980s. 'Art education here is forward-thinking, and there's such a hybridization of culture in this city that it can't help but be influential.'

'If London art colleges symbolize a kind of creative catalyst, their other secret is the liberty each course gives its students,' says Wilson. 'It might sound contrived, but the freedom we allow students is integral to our success. All you can do is push them to work hard; you can't teach creativity.'

ABOVE: *Andrew Groves.*
Photo Jonathan de Villiers.

# ANDREW GROVES

| | |
|---|---|
| Date of birth: | 27 February 1968 |
| Design school attended: | Central Saint Martins College of Art and Design – MA |
| Label started: | February 1997 |
| Label's philosophy: | Constantly to push fashion forwards into new and unexpected areas while using old artisan techniques in construction and cut |
| Personal philosophy: | Fashion should constantly try to overthrow the establishment, to challenge the norm and fight against complacency |
| Signature look: | Sharp tailoring with intricate cutting techniques |
| In one word: | Modern |
| Inspiration source: | Every six months, I sit in a library for two solid weeks and read and absorb everything |
| Most inspirational person: | No one person really, I just try to inspire myself through constant research |
| Design turn-on: | Getting such strong reactions from the cut and construction of 3 metres of cloth. Making people think more about the strength of dress in society |

# FAKE LONDON
Desirée Mejer

| | |
|---|---|
| Date of birth: | 11 November 1968 |
| Design school attended: | No formal fashion training |
| Label started: | April 1995 |
| Label's philosophy: | Do unique things for intelligent people |
| Signature look: | Union Jack sweater made of recycled cashmere. Sweaters in non-traditional colours |
| In one word: | Interesting |
| Inspiration source: | Everyday life |
| Most inspirational person: | My mother, for teaching me the principles of style |
| Design turn-on: | The potential for creating instant happiness based on futile, overrated things. The amount of information needed to be condensed in one perfect piece |

BELOW: *Desirée Mejer.*
Photo Jonathan de Villiers.

ABOVE: *Deborah Milner.*
Photo Jonathan de Villiers.

# DEBORAH MILNER

| | |
|---|---|
| Date of birth: | 1 March 1964 |
| Design school attended: | Central Saint Martins College of Art and Design Royal College of Art |
| Label started: | March 1992 |
| Label's philosophy: | Explore. Have a good sense of proportion and pursue dreams |
| Signature look: | Dress made of Rigelene boning photographed by Mario Testino for the *Sunday Times* Style magazine |
| In one word: | Sculptural |
| Inspiration source: | Modern art and sculpture; interested in the exploration of forms and ideas, sculptural and painterly techniques |
| Most inspirational person: | My friend Lisa who, when growing up in a small town, didn't follow trends but set them. She was a total original and would not accept the mundane or mediocre |
| Design turn-on: | The process of having an idea and then working through until it actually materializes. Working in a sculptural way; making paper sculpture on a stand, cutting it up, making a pattern, making my own shoulder-pad shape, getting the perfect colour fabric |

# ELVIS JESUS AND CO. COUTURE
Kurt Levi Jones & Helen Littler

| | |
|---|---|
| Date of birth: | KLJ: 19 December 1968 HL: 28 September 1969 |
| Design school attended: | KLJ: Salford University and Ravensbourne College HL: University of Manchester |
| Label started: | 1997 |
| Label's philosophy: | Live, learn and be fabulous |
| Signature look: | Bubble-gum pink sari dress |
| In one word: | Gigi |
| Inspiration source: | Life |
| Most inspirational person: | KLJ: Toyah has been a constant influence. Her use of cultural and tribal imagery to create constantly changing characters through costume and make-up inspired me to start designing HL: Cecil Beaton – because you can't live without elegance |
| Design turn-on: | Glamour, glitter, fashion and fame |

BELOW: *Kurt Levi Jones and Helen Littler, Elvis Jesus and Co. Couture.*
Photo Jonathan de Villiers.

# GHARANI STROK
Nargess Gharani & Vanja Strok

| | |
|---|---|
| Date of birth: | NG: 8 July 1970 |
| | VS: 1 October 1969 |
| Design school attended: | NG: Surrey Institute of Art and Design – Epsom Campus |
| | VS: Kingston University |
| Label started: | June 1995 |
| Label's philosophy: | We create contemporary clothes in the spirit of our time where different cultures and backgrounds are mixed together, along with the old and new. This is reflected in our eclectic mix of multi-textured fabrics, yet understated and feminine pieces |
| Personal philosophy: | To create individual clothes that we would want to wear. Preferring to let the fabrics dictate the shapes rather than following any rules or trends, otherwise things are too fashionable and they do not last |
| Signature look: | Dainty slip dresses and separates held together with just one seam, therefore flattering most body shapes. Focusing on special fabrics and subtle details |
| In one word: | Us |
| Inspiration source: | Fabrics; travel; cultural books; Helena Christensen; ourselves; music; tough chicks |
| Most inspirational person: | Mum |
| Design turn-on: | Tits and ass and Rock'n'Roll |

# SUTURE
Tom Adams & Philip Delamore

| | |
|---|---|
| Date of birth: | TA: 18 August 1961 |
| | PD: 9 July 1968 |
| Design school attended: | TA: Loughborough University – Fine Art BA (Hons); Royal Academy – Printing MA |
| | PD: Cheltenham & Gloucester College of Higher Education – Fashion and Printed Textiles BA (Hons) |
| Label started: | December 1995 |
| Label's philosophy: | FAST – Fashion, Art, Science, Technology |
| Signature look: | Visceral print, clean, modern, uncluttered |
| In one word: | Modern |
| Inspiration source: | The viewfinder of Spike Walker's (the photomicrographer with whom we collaborate on print images) Zeiss Microscope |
| Design turn-on: | Problem solving. Working with restrictions. The process of working with the body both systematically and anatomically. The idea of the body as the ultimate piece of design. Working with recurrent patterns within nature. Possibilities of collaboration |

# TRISTAN WEBBER

Date of birth:             22 March 1972

Design school attended:    Central Saint Martins College of
                           Art and Design – BA Hons and MA

Label started:             April 1997

Label's philosophy:        To develop a personalized mode of
                           experience that commands a
                           heightened sensuality within oneself
                           and an augmented perfection of the
                           wearer's character. To redistribute
                           recognized forms of cutting and
                           construction that explore the
                           interior/negative spaces of the human
                           make-up within a context of modern
                           emotions and intellectual requirements

Personal philosophy:       Treating the body as a malleable form
                           of expression via creative surgery to
                           result in mental adjustment

Signature look:            An intercut garment that maps the
                           zones of internal power, and
                           sensualizes the dermal layer

In one word:               Harderfastersilent (Stealth)

Inspiration source:        The reaction of a woman wearing
                           the clothes

Most inspirational person: Riné Couture (Corrine Sifflet-Seymour)

Design turn-on:            The facility to rebuild

## Y.M.C. (YOU MUST CREATE)
Frazer Moss & Jimmy Collins

Date of birth:             FM: 15 January 1966
                           JC: 29 March 1968

Design school attended:    No formal design training

Label started:             Autumn 1996

Label's philosophy:        To produce a modern, functional
                           collection for men and women

Signature look:            To create clothes that I'd wear myself

In one word:               Modern

Inspiration source:        Influences drawn from all aspects of
                           post-50s living and design (graphics,
                           architecture and the arts); boot fairs; art
                           & graphics reference books

Most inspirational person: Pierre Cardin for introducing fashion
                           as a lifestyle

Design turn-on:            Seeing people on the street wearing
                           Y.M.C.

*LEFT: Tristan Webber.*
Photo Jonathan de Villiers.

*ABOVE: Frazer Moss and
Jimmy Collins, Y.M.C.*
Photo Jonathan de Villiers.

# FASHION DIRECTORY

*All shops known by the designer's name are alphabetized under the last name of the designer. Only one branch of each company is listed.*

**A La Mode**
36 Hans Crescent
SW1
0171 584 2133
*International designer labels*

**Agent Provocateur**
6 Broadwick Street
W1
0171 439 0229
*Naughty underwear*

**Ally Capellino**
66 Sloane Avenue
SW3
0171 591 8201
*See page 164*

**Bill Amberg**
10 Chepstow Road
W2
0171 727 3560
*Designer bags and furniture*

**American Retro**
35 Old Compton Street
W1
0171 734 3477
*Accessories, cards, gifts*

**Antoni & Alison**
43 Roseberry Avenue
EC1
0171 833 2141
*Vacuum packed souvenir clothing and accessories*

**Jacques Azagury**
50 Knightsbridge
SW1
0171 235 0799
*Modern eveningwear*

**Joseph Azagury**
73 Knightsbridge
SW1
0171 259 6887
*Shoes, evening bags*

**Solange Azagury-Partridge**
171 Westbourne Grove
W11
0171 792 0197
*Jewelry – gold and precious stones*

**Fred Bare**
118 Columbia Road
E2
0171 739 4612
*Youthful hats; shop open only on Sunday*

**Slim Barrett**
Studio 6
Shepperton House
Shepperton Road
N1
0171 354 9393
*See pages 124–125*

**Blackout II**
51 Endell Street
WC2
0171 240 5006
*Kitschy vintage clothing and accessories*

**Manolo Blahnik**
49–51 Old Church Street
SW3
0171 352 8622
*See page 52*

**Selina Blow**
42 Elizabeth Street
SW1
0171 730 2449
*Scarves, bags and her own designs*

**Ozwald Boateng**
9 Vigo Street
W1
0171 734 6868
*See page 97*

**Bond**
10 Newburgh Street
W1
0171 437 0079
*Streetwear and skatewear*

**Browns**
23–27 South Molton Street
W1
0171 491 7833
*Designer labels*

**Browns Focus**
38–39 South Molton Street
W1
0171 629 0666
*Young designer labels*

**Burro**
19a Floral Street
WC2
0171 240 5120
*Streetwise menswear*

**Butler & Wilson**
189 Fulham Road
SW3
0171 352 3045
*Costume jewelry*

**Cashmere by Design**
64 Neal Street
WC2
0171 240 3652
*Cashmere designs with zest*

**Caroline Charles**
56–57 Beauchamp Place

SW3
0171 225 3197
*See pages 136–137*

**Cenci**
31 Monmouth Street
WC2
0171 836 1400
*Desirable second-hand clothing*

**The Changing Room**
Thomas Neal's Centre
Earlham Street
WC2
0171 379 4158
*Clothing, accessories, interior design*

**Jimmy Choo**
20 Motcomb Street
SW1
0171 235 6008
*Delicate, stylish shoes*

**Cobra & Bellamy**
149 Sloane Street
SW1
0171 730 9993
*Jewelry – silver, amber and jet*

**Cornucopia**
12 Upper Tachbrook Street
SW1
0171 828 5752
*Vintage clothing, 1890s to 1950s*

**Paul Costelloe**
156 Brompton Road
SW3
0171 589 9480
*Clothes with a country appeal*

**Patrick Cox**
8 Symons Street
SW3
*See page 70*

**The Cross**
141 Portland Road
W11
0171 727 6760
*Hats, bags and scarves*

**Dickins & Jones**
224–244 Regent Street
W1
0171 734 7070
*Department store; useful for basics*

**Diesel**
43 Earlham Street
WC2
0171 497 5543
*Space-age clubwear*

**The Dispensary**
25 Pembridge Road

W11
0171 221 9290
*The latest trendy labels*

**Dr Martens Dept Store**
1–4 King Street
WC2
0171 497 1460
*Doc Martens from head to toe*

**Duffer of St George**
29 Shorts Gardens
WC2
0171 379 4660
*Cool retro designs*

**Egg**
36 Kinnerton Street
SW1
0171 235 9315
*Arty clothes – beyond fashion*

**Erickson Beamon**
38 Elizabeth Street
SW1
0171 259 0202
*See pages 124–125*

**Timothy Everest**
32 Elder Street
E1
0171 377 5770
*See page 95*

**Nicole Farhi**
158 Bond Street
W1
0171 499 8368
*See page 67*

**Favourbrook**
18–21 Piccadilly Arcade
SW1
0171 491 2337
*Romantic clothes for peacock males; also womenswear*

**Janet Fitch**
25a Old Compton Street
W1
0171 240 6332
*Jewelry from young British designers*

**Ghost**
36 Ledbury Road
W11
0171 229 1057
*See page 166*

**Gina**
189 Sloane Street
SW1
0171 235 2932
*Well-crafted, stylish shoes*

**Olowu Golding**
30 Artesian Road
W2

0171 229 7120
*Impeccably finished clothes and handmade shoes*

**Graham & Green**
10 Elgin Crescent
W11
0171 727 4594
*Well chosen designer labels in clothing, accessories and jewelry*

**Lulu Guinness**
66 Ledbury Road
W11
0171 221 9686
*Pretty, witty bags*

**Dinny Hall**
200 Westbourne Grove
W11
0171 792 3913
*Modern jewelry*

**Katharine Hamnett**
20 Sloane Street
SW1
0171 823 1002
*See page 74*

**Harrods**
87 Brompton Road
SW1
0171 730 1234
*Wide selection of designer labels*

**Harvey Nichols**
109–125 Knightsbridge
SW1
0171 235 5000
*Fashion department store; every designer label*

**Anouska Hempel**
2 Pond Place
SW3
0171 589 4191
*See pages 138–139*

**Anya Hindmarch**
15–17 Pont Street
SW1
0171 838 9177
*See pages 138–139*

**Home**
39 Beak Street
W1
0171 287 3708
*Streetwear, surfwear, skatewear*

**Emma Hope**
33 Amwell Street
EC1
0171 833 2367
*17th-century-style shoes in rich fabrics*

**Margaret Howell**
29 Beauchamp Place

SW3
0171 584 5770
*See page 81*

**Idol**
15 Ingestre Place
W1
0171 439 8537
*Special-occasion wear with a medieval look*

**Betty Jackson**
311 Brompton Road
SW3
0171 589 7884
*See page 80*

**Richard James**
31 Savile Row
W1
0171 434 0605
*See page 94*

**Jones**
13–15 Floral Street
WC2
0171 240 8312
*Avant-garde designer labels for men*

**Stephen Jones**
36 Great Queen Street
WC2
0171 242 0770
*See page 78*

**Joseph**
77 Fulham Road
SW3
0171 823 9500
*Joseph Ettedgui's fashion emporium*

**Ninivah Khomo**
5 Beauchamp Place
SW3
0171 591 0112
*Animal prints – on women's clothing and soft furnishings*

**Koh Samui**
65 Monmouth Street
WC2
0171 240 4280
*Cutting-edge designer labels*

**Kokon to Zai**
57 Greek Street
W1
0171 434 1316
*Kooky designer labels and records*

**Lawrence Corner**
62–64 Hampstead Road
NW1
0171 813 1010
*Army surplus to mix and match*

**Liberty**
210–221 Regent Street

W1
0171 734 1234
*London's best selection of young British designs*

**The Library**
268 Brompton road
SW3
0171 589 6569
*Menswear plus books*

**Merc**
17–19 Ganton Street
W1
0171 734 1469
*Skinheads and mods shop here*

**Merchant of Europe**
232 Portobello Road
W11
0171 221 4203
*Vintage clothing*

**Mimi**
309 King's Road
SW3
0171 349 9699
*Feminine contemporary designer clothing*

**Johnny Moke**
396 King's Road
SW10
0171 351 2232
*Quirky, elegant men's and women's shoes*

**Rachel Trevor Morgan**
18 Crown Passage
King Street
SW1
0171 839 8927
*Showstopping Ascot hats*

**Mulberry**
41–42 New Bond Street
W1
0171 491 3900
*Clothing, leather accessories and interior furnishings*

**R Newbold**
7–8 Langley Court
WC2
0171 240 5068
*Military-type uniforms and workwear*

**Oguri**
64 Ledbury Road
W11
0171 792 3847
*Fashionable clothing of today and yesterday*

**Bruce Oldfield**
27 Beauchamp Place
SW3
0171 584 1363
*See pages 136–139*

**Pellicano**
63 South Molton Street
W1
0171 629 2205
*Designer labels*

**Mark Powell**
17 Newburgh Street (first floor)
W1
0171 287 5498
*See page 96*

**Question Air**
38 Floral Street
WC2
0171 836 8220
*Selected designer labels*

**Red or Dead**
38 Kensington High Street
W14
0171 937 1649
*Wayne and Geraldine Hemingway's famous streetwear and shoe store*

**John Richmond**
2 Newburgh Street
W1
0171 734 5782
*Directional clubwear and denim*

**Savoy Tailors Guild**
164 New Bond Street
W1
0171 408 1680
*Menswear basics plus selected designer labels*

**Selfridges**
400 Oxford Street
W1
0171 629 1234
*Department store with highly praised fashion floors*

**Shop**
Basement, 4 Brewer Street
W1
0171 437 1259
*Soho's funkiest fashion venue*

**Slam City Skates**
16 Neal's Yard
WC2
0171 240 0928
*Skatewear and sportswear*

**Paul Smith**
40–44 Floral Street
WC2
0171 379 7133
*See page 64*

**Space NK Apothecary**
Thomas Neal's Centre
Earlham Street
WC2

0171 379 7030
*Unusual beauty products from around the world*

**Tomasz Starzewski**
177–178 Sloane Street
SW1
0171 235 4526
*See pages 136–137*

**Steinberg & Tolkien**
193 King's Road
SW3
0171 376 3660
*Vintage clothing, costume jewelry and accessories*

**Sub Couture**
204 Kensington Park Road
W11
0171 229 5434
*Own-label clubwear plus covetable selection of accessories from other designers*

**Tokio**
309 Brompton Road
SW3
0171 823 7310
*Up-to-the-minute designer labels*

**Philip Treacy**
69 Elizabeth Street
SW1
0171 259 9605
*See page 48*

**295**
295 Portobello Road
W10
No phone
*Bargain second-hand clothing*

**Vent**
178a Westbourne Grove
W11
No telephone
*Vintage clothing and bric-a-brac*

**Vexed Generation**
First floor, 3 Berwick Street
W1
0171 287 6224
*Environmentally kind clothing*

**Georgina von Etzdorf**
50 Burlington Arcade
W1
0171 409 7789
*See pages 168–169*

**Voyage**
115 Fulham Road
SW3
0171 823 9581
*High-cost hippie wear*

**Amanda Wakeley**
80 Fulham Road
SW3
0171 584 4009
*See page 76*

**Catherine Walker**
65 Sydney Street
SW3
0171 352 4626
*See pages 136–139*

**Vivienne Westwood**
6 Davies Street
W1
0171 629 3757
*See page 30*

**Whistles**
12 St Christopher's Place
W1
0171 487 4484
*Own label and designer merchandise for young professionals*

## MARKETS

**Brick Lane Market**
Bethnal Green Road
Cheshire Street and Brick Lane
E2
*Junk and fleamarket finds*

**Camden Lock**
Chalk Farm Road
NW1
*Antiques and objets d'art*

**Camden Market**
Camden High Street
NW1
*Young fashion and ethnic knick-knacks*

**Columbia Road Market**
Columbia Road
E3
*Flowers and bric-à-brac*

**Petticoat Lane**
Middlesex and Wentworth Streets
E1
*Cheap and cheerful market finds*

**Portobello Green Arcade**
281 Portobello Road
W10
*Fashion and handicrafts*

**Portobello Market**
Portobello Road
W11
*Clothes and antiques*

**Tom Adams** *See* **Suture**

**Agent Provocateur** (Joseph Corre and Serena Rees) Designers. Joseph Corre (b. 1967, London, England) worked for nine years for his mother, Vivienne Westwood, before launching the lingerie boutique Agent Provocateur with Serena Rees (b. 1968, London, England) in Soho in 1994. Corre and Rees have designed theatre costumes and a uniform for the waitresses at Café de Paris in London. A mini version of the Soho shop opened at the Fiorucci department store in Milan in 1996 and a further branch was established in London in 1998.

**Ally Capellino** (Alison Lloyd) Designer. Born 1956 in London, England. After studying Fashion and Textiles at Middlesex Polytechnic, Lloyd began working at Courtaulds Central Design Studio in London in 1978. She founded Ally Capellino one year later, specializing in hats and accessories. In 1980 she produced her first womenswear collection. Ally Capellino Menswear was launched in 1986, followed by the Hearts of Oak sportswear line in 1990 and Mini Capellino childrenswear in 1991. The ao range, featuring signature Ally Capellino styles at affordable prices, was introduced in 1996, replacing Hearts of Oak. In 1997 the Ally Capellino flagship store was opened in Sloane Avenue, Chelsea.

**Nigel Atkinson** Fabric designer. Born 1964 in London, England. Atkinson studied Textile Design at Winchester School of Art. In 1987 he established a handprinting workshop, designing fabric for international fashion houses, including Alaïa, Gigli and Ferretti. In 1994 he launched a highly successful accessories label and in 1997 brought out the Nigel Atkinson Interior Textile fabric line.

**Slim Barrett** Jewelry designer. Born 1960 in County Galway, Ireland. Barrett studied Fine Art at the Regional Technical College, Galway, and arrived in 1982 in London, where he began to design jewelry. He has received commissions for accessories from John Galliano, Katharine Hamnett and Claude Montana, among others. He presented his first collection in 1983.

**Antonio Berardi** Designer. Born 1968 in Grantham, Lincolnshire, England. While still a student at Central St Martins College of Art and Design in London, Berardi began designing for John Galliano. In 1994, his graduation collection was bought by Liberty and A La Mode. He launched his own design label later that year and in 1995 held his first catwalk show. Berardi has worked with Stephen Jones, Manolo Blahnik and Anya Hindmarch, among others.

**Manolo Blahnik** Shoe designer. Born 1943 in Santa Cruz, Canary Islands. Blahnik studied Literature in Geneva, then moved to Paris in 1968 to study Art at the Ecole du Louvre. In 1970 he went to New York, where he sent a portfolio of his sketches to a number of fashion editors, including Diana Vreeland, who encouraged him to design shoes. A year later he moved to London, where in 1973 he opened his first boutique, Zapata. Blahnik has collaborated with many of the world's most successful fashion houses.

**Pamela Blundell** *See* **Copperwheat Blundell**

**Ozwald Boateng** Designer/bespoke tailor. Born 1967 in London, England. After a one-year fashion course at Southgate Technical College, Boateng met the legendary Savile Row tailor Tommy Nutter, who inspired him to take up tailoring. In 1994 he had his first catwalk show in Paris and the following year opened his own bespoke tailoring shop in Vigo Street. As well as 'bespoke couture' – a fusion of fashion design and traditional tailoring – Boateng produces ready-to-wear collections which he shows twice a year in Paris. In 1996 he won the Trophées de la Mode Best Male Designer Award.

**Joe Casely-Hayford** Designer. Born 1956 in Kent, England. Casely-Hayford first gained experience at a tailoring establishment in Savile Row, London, before attending the Tailor and Cutter Academy in 1974. From 1975 he studied Fashion at St Martins School of Art, followed by History of Art at the Institute of Contemporary Arts in London. In 1983 he began producing collections for both men and women. Since 1993 Casely-Hayford has created best-selling lines of womenswear for Top Shop. He is also known for his work with rock groups and singers.

**Hussein Chalayan** Designer. Born 1970 in Nicosia, Cyprus. Chalayan graduated in Fashion from Central St Martins College of Art and Design in London in 1993. His final-year collection was featured by Browns, a leading designer store, and in 1994 he launched his own label, presenting his first solo collection in the same year.

**Caroline Charles** Designer. Born 1942 in Cairo, Egypt. Charles studied at Swindon School of Art in Wiltshire until 1960, when she began an apprenticeship with Michael Sherard before joining Mary Quant as a designer. Charles launched her own house in 1963. In 1994 her flagship store opened in Bond Street, London.

**Suzanne Clements** *See* **Clements Ribeiro**

**Clements Ribeiro** (Suzanne Clements and Inacio Ribeiro) Designers. Clements (b. 1968, Surrey, England) and Ribeiro (b. 1963, Itapacerica, Brazil) both worked as designers before they met at Central St Martins College of Art and Design in London. Following their graduation in 1991, the couple married and moved to Brazil, where they established a design consultancy firm. On their return to London in 1993, they started their own label, presenting their first collection for Spring/Summer 1994. In 1995 Clements Ribeiro collaborated with the Scottish firm Barrie Knitwear to produce garments in cashmere. The following year saw the introduction of a range of shoes and the launch of a womenswear line for the chainstore Dorothy Perkins.

**Jimmy Collins** *See* **Y.M.C.**

**Jasper Conran** Designer. Born 1959 in London, England. After graduating from Parsons School of Design in New York in 1977, Conran worked briefly for Fiorucci. Later the same year he returned to London, where he designed womenswear for the New York department store Henri Bendel and was employed as a consultant by Wallis, for whom he produced the 'Special Label'. In 1978 he launched his first womenswear collection, adding menswear and accessories from 1988. Since 1990 he has worked extensively in the theatre, on set and costume designs. In 1996 he began designing the J range of womenswear for the department store Debenhams.

**Lee Copperwheat.** *See* **Copperwheat Blundell**

**Copperwheat Blundell** (Lee Copperwheat and Pamela Blundell) Designers. Copperwheat (b. 1966, Welwyn Garden City, Hertfordshire, England) trained in tailoring in Northampton before working for two years for Aquascutum. In 1986 he began studying Fashion and Tailoring at the London College of Fashion. Then followed three years at the sportswear company Passenger, after which he worked freelance for Margaret Howell and Jasper Conran, among others. Blundell (b. 1967 in Hook, Hampshire, England) studied Fashion at Southampton University and then attended Epsom School of Art and Design. Following her studies, she became assistant to John Flett and designed his diffusion line. The two designers met while they were teaching at Central St Martins College of Art and Design in the early 1990s, and the Copperwheat Blundell label was launched in 1993. Blundell creates the company's womenswear while Copperwheat designs the menswear lines.

**Joseph Corre** *See* **Agent Provocateur**

**Patrick Cox** Shoe designer. Born 1963 in Edmonton, Canada. Cox trained at Cordwainers College in London. As a student he designed shoes for Vivienne Westwood and received commissions from Body Map and John Galliano. In 1991 he established his flagship store in London. Cox launched his signature Wannabe loafers for men and women in 1993. In 1994 Patrick Cox was given the 'Accessory Designer of the Year' award.

**Neisha Crosland** Textile designer. Born 1960 in London, England. Crosland studied Textiles at Camberwell School of Arts, and took an MA in Printed Textiles at the Royal College of Art, graduating in 1986. Since then she has successfully developed fabric designs for leading international designers including Calvin Klein, Rifat Ozbek and Christian Lacroix. She launched her own scarf collection in 1994.

**Helen David English Eccentrics** Textile and clothing designer. Born 1955 in Brighton, England. David trained in Fashion and Textiles at Camberwell School of Arts and St Martins School of Art, graduating in 1977. In 1983 she founded the company English Eccentrics, which launched its first collection the following year. In 1997, David added her own name to her label.

**Philip Delamore** *See* **Suture**

**Ben de Lisi** Designer. Born 1955 in Long Island, New York, USA. De Lisi studied Sculpture and Painting at the Pratt Institute of Fine Arts in Brooklyn from 1973 to 1977. Two years later he created his first menswear collection. In 1982 he moved to London to establish a French restaurant in Belgravia, but turned again to fashion in 1984, when he produced a small collection of womenswear. In 1994 and 1995 he was voted 'British Glamour Designer of the Year' and held his first catwalk show in March 1995.

**Jonathan Docherty** *See* **Georgina von Etzdorf**

**Mark Eley** *See* **Eley Kishimoto**

**Eley Kishimoto** (Mark Eley and Wakako Kishimoto) Textile designers. A husband-and-wife team. Eley (b. 1968, South Wales) graduated from Brighton Polytechnic in 1990 after studying Fashion and Textiles. Kishimoto (b. 1965, Kobe, Japan) graduated in 1992 from Central St Martins College of Art and Design, where she specialized in Print on both the BA and MA Fashion and Textiles course. Their textile design company was formed in 1992 and includes among its clients Joe Casely-Hayford, Hussein Chalayan and Alexander McQueen. Eley Kishimoto launched its first collection for Autumn/Winter 1996–97.

**Elvis Jesus and Co. Couture** (Kurt Levi Jones and Helen Littler) Designers. Jones (b. 1968, Birmingham, England) trained in Fashion and Textiles at Salford University and Ravensbourne College until 1993. Littler (b. 1969, Manchester, England) studied

Clothing Design Technology at Manchester University, graduating in 1992. The two met in 1988 at a club in Manchester and launched their label in 1997, showing their first collection in Spring/Summer of that year. Elvis Jesus and Co. Couture work from both Manchester and London.

**English Eccentrics** *See* **Helen David English Eccentrics**

**Karen Erickson** *See* **Erickson Beamon**

**Erickson Beamon** (Karen Erickson and Vicki L. Sarge) Jewelry designers. Erickson (b. Detroit, USA) and Sarge (b. 1954, Detroit, USA) had no formal training. Their partnership began in New York in 1983 and in 1985 Sarge started a branch of the company in London. The first UK Erickson Beamon shop opened in Elizabeth Street, Belgravia, at the end of 1994.

**Timothy Everest** Designer/bespoke tailor. Born 1961 in Southampton, England. Everest served his apprenticeship in the early 1980s with the tailor Tommy Nutter and the retailer Malcolm Levine. His business is based in Spitalfields, London. He produced his first collection in 1993.

**Fake London** (Desirée Mejer) Designer. Born 1968 near Cadiz in Spain. Mejer came to London in 1992 and, with no formal training, set up her label in 1995. Her first collection was launched during the Autumn/Winter 1997 season.

**Nicole Farhi** Designer. Born 1949 in Nice, France. Farhi studied Fashion Design in Paris and began her career as a freelance designer. She moved to London in the early 1970s, joining Stephen Marks to found the French Connection label. Farhi established her own womenswear company in 1983 and in 1989 created a line of clothing for men. The Nicole Farhi flagship store opened in 1994 in New Bond Street, London, and was followed by a menswear shop in Covent Garden in the following year.

**David Fielden** Designer. Born 1951 in the Lake District, England. Originally trained in Theatre and Costume Design at Birmingham College of Art, Fielden joined the Ballet Rambert as a dancer and choreographer but changed the course of his career when he began to sell vintage clothing in Antiquarius on the King's Road. In 1977 he set up his own shop on the King's Road, designing wedding dresses and, subsequently, eveningwear.

**Naomi Filmer** Jewelry designer. Born 1969 in London, England. Filmer graduated from the Royal College of Art in 1993 with an MA in Metalwork and Jewelry. She has collaborated with Hussein Chalayan, Julien MacDonald and Tristan Webber. She launched her first collection when she worked with Chalayan on his 1994 catwalk show.

**Andrew Fionda** *See* **Pearce Fionda**

**Bella Freud** Designer. Born 1961 in London, England. Freud studied tailoring in Rome, at the Accademia di Costuma e di Moda and at the Instituto Mariotti Tailoring School, graduating in 1985. As a student she designed shoes and knitwear for a number of clients. In 1990 she launched her own label, showing her first catwalk collection in 1993.

**John Galliano** Designer. Born 1960 in Gibraltar. Galliano moved to London at the age of six. He studied Fashion at St Martins School of Art and in 1984 his final-year collection, 'Les Incroyables', was immediately bought by Browns. The John Galliano label was started in 1984 and Galliano presented his first collection for Spring/Summer 1985. He has won the 'British Designer of the Year' award three times. In 1995 Galliano was appointed Head Designer at Givenchy. He moved to the house of Dior in 1997.

**Owen Gaster** Designer. Born 1969 in Beirut, Lebanon, to British parents. Gaster graduated from Epsom College of Art and Design in 1992. He produced his first catwalk collection for Autumn/Winter 1994, attracting such clients as the international chain Joseph and Galeries Lafayette in Paris.

**Nargess Gharani** *See* **Gharani Strok**

**Gharani Strok** (Nargess Gharani and Vanja Strok) Designers. Gharani (b. 1970, Teheran, Iran) trained at Surrey Institute of Art and Design, graduating in 1992. Strok (b. 1969, Zagreb, Croatia) studied at Kingston University and graduated in 1994. They started their label in 1995 and launched their first collection in the same year.

**Ghost** (Tanya Sarne) Designer. Born 1940s in London, England. Sarne studied History and Psychology at Sussex University from 1964 to 1967 and first worked in fashion as a model. After travelling in the United States, South America and Europe, she started a business in 1976 importing Peruvian alpaca knitwear. Sarne introduced the Scandinavian labels In Wear and Laize Adzer to the UK market and in 1978 established her own sportswear line, Miz. In 1984 she launched the Ghost range.

**Elspeth Gibson** Designer. Born 1963 in Nottingham, England. Gibson graduated from Nottinghamshire College of Design in 1984. She embarked on her career at Zandra Rhodes in 1985, moving in 1995 to Monix, where she became head of design. She left to set up her own label in 1996, launching her first collection in the same year.

**Andrew Groves** Designer. Born 1967 in Maidstone, Kent, England. Groves graduated from Central St Martins College of Art and Design in 1997 and started his label that same year, launching his first collection in February 1997.

**Abe Hamilton** Designer. Born 1962 in Manchester. Originally a chef, Hamilton went on to study Art and Fashion at Middlesex Polytechnic. His final degree collection stimulated interest from fashion editors, photographers and film-makers who used his clothes in their creative work. In 1990 he launched his debut collection. He presented his first catwalk show in 1993 and was voted 'New Generation Designer of the Year'.

**Katharine Hamnett** Designer. Born 1948 in Gravesend, England. Hamnett graduated from St Martins School of Art in 1969 and started the Tuttabankem label with Anne Buck. From 1975 she worked freelance until she established her own house in 1979. Her famous 'Choose Life' T-shirt collection was launched in 1983 and two years later she participated in the 1985 'Big Five' fashion show in Tokyo. Hamnett promotes the use of environmentally friendly fabrics in her designs.

**Anouska Hempel** No personal or career details available. The Anouska Hempel company was founded in 1988.

**Samantha Heskia** Handbag designer. Born 1967 in London, England. Heskia attended Wimbledon School of Art until 1985 and then studied Interior Architecture at Chelsea School of Art, graduating in 1988. She began her career as an interior designer and in the early 1990s created sets for a number of films. She turned to designing handbags in 1995.

**Anya Hindmarch** Handbag designer. Born 1968 in Burnham-on-Crouch, England. Hindmarch had no formal training in design. The success of a handbag design commissioned by *Harpers & Queen* allowed her to start her own business in 1987, at the age of 19. In 1993 the first Anya Hindmarch shop opened in Walton Street, London, followed in 1995 by a branch in Hong Kong and in 1997 by a second London store.

**Margaret Howell** Designer. Born 1946 in Surrey, England. On graduating from Goldsmiths College of Art in London in 1969, Howell began to design accessories which were featured in *Vogue*. In 1970 she established a studio in Blackheath where she produced both menswear and womenswear. Her flagship store opened in London in 1980, followed by branches in London, Paris and Japan.

**Betty Jackson** Designer. Born 1940 in Backup, Lancashire, England. Jackson studied at Birmingham College of Art until 1971, when she moved to London and worked as a freelance designer. In 1973 she joined Wendy Dagworthy, moving to Quorum in 1975. Jackson founded her own company in 1981. In 1985 she was awarded the title 'British Designer of the Year'. She supplements her womenswear collections with lines in knitwear, swimwear and accessories.

**Richard James** Designer/bespoke tailor. Born 1953 in Ely, Cambridgeshire, England. James studied Photography at Brighton Art College, graduating in 1978. He gained experience in tailoring by working for a number of years at Browns in London. The first Richard James shop opened in Savile Row in 1992 and a second was established in New York in 1997. His clients include Liam and Noel Gallagher, Elton John and Madonna.

**Kurt Levi Jones** *See* **Elvis Jesus and Co. Couture**

**Stephen Jones** Milliner. Born 1957 in West Kirby, Liverpool, England. After a period at High Wycombe School of Art, Jones studied Fashion Design at St Martins School of Art. He graduated in 1979 and in 1980 opened his first millinery salon in Covent Garden. His career flourished in the 1980s with commissions from pop groups such as Spandau Ballet, Culture Club and the Rolling Stones. In 1984 he began working for Gaultier, Mugler and Comme des Garçons in Paris and since then has collaborated with London-based and international designers, including Berardi, Galliano, Dior, Joop!, Ozbek and Westwood. In 1990 he launched a number of accessory and diffusion lines.

**Lainey Keogh** Knitwear designer. Born 1957 in County Dublin, Ireland. Keogh began her career in fashion by knitting sweaters for her friends. In 1984 she started producing knitwear commercially and in 1986 set up her own knitwear design company, receiving the Prix de Coeur at the Monte Carlo fashion awards in 1989. Her first catwalk show took place in 1994.

**Wakako Kishimoto** *See* **Eley Kishimoto**

**Sherald Lamden** *See* **Seraph**

**Helen Littler** *See* **Elvis Jesus and Co. Couture**

**Alison Lloyd** *See* **Ally Capellino**

**Julien MacDonald** Knitwear designer. Born 1972 in Merthyr Tydfil, Wales. MacDonald graduated from the Royal College of Art in June 1996. His graduation collection was seen by Karl Lagerfeld and he was offered a work placement at Chanel in Paris where, within two weeks, he was appointed knitwear designer for Chanel ready-to-wear. MacDonald launched his first collection in 1997. He has also worked with Alexander McQueen, Koji Tatsuno and Antonio Berardi.

**Stella McCartney** Designer. Born 1971 in London, England. At the age of 15, McCartney worked for Christian Lacroix in Paris on his 'Premier Couture' collection. After completing her A levels in 1987, she took a year off to gain further experience in the fashion industry by assisting Betty Jackson and working for *Vogue*. She studied Fashion Design at Central St Martins College of Art and Design, graduating in 1995 and moving on to work with Savile Row tailor Edward Sexton. In 1996 she was appointed chief designer at Chloé.

**Alexander McQueen** Designer. Born 1969 in London, England. McQueen was apprenticed to the Savile Row tailors Anderson & Sheppard at the age of 16. He then worked for Gieves & Hawkes, another Savile Row establishment, and for the theatrical costumiers Bermans & Nathans. In 1979 McQueen moved to Japan to join Koji Tatsuno and was also employed by the house of Gigli in Milan. On his return to London he took an MA course in Fashion at Central St Martins College of Art and Design. McQueen launched his career in 1992 with his graduation collection, which was immediately bought by stylist Isabella Blow. In 1997 he became the youngest designer to win the 'Designer of the Year' award and was appointed head designer at Givenchy.

**Desirée Mejer** See **Fake London**

**Deborah Milner** Designer. Born 1964 in Surrey, England. Milner graduated from Central St Martins College of Art and Design in 1987 and established a couture atelier in 1991. She showed a small collection for the first time in 1993.

**Frazer Moss** See **Y.M.C.**

**Sonja Nuttall** Designer. Born 1964 in Liverpool, England. Nuttall studied Fashion Design and Textiles at Central St Martins College of Art and Design. On her graduation in 1991, she worked for Norman Hartnell and Gina Fratini and was awarded a scholarship for 'Most Prominent New Designer'. She returned to St Martins in 1992 to complete an MA in Fashion Design. Since launching her first collection in 1994, Nuttall has worked as a design consultant for Debenhams, Margaret Howell and Peterson of Dublin.

**Bruce Oldfield** Designer. Born 1950 in London, England. Oldfield trained as a teacher at Sheffield City Polytechnic, graduating in 1971. He then transferred to Ravensbourne College of Art's Fashion and Textiles degree course, and, in the following year, to the Fashion and Design course at St Martins School of Art. In 1973 he began a period as a freelance designer, creating collections for Liberty and a line for Henri Bendel of New York. The first Bruce Oldfield collection was presented in 1975. In 1978 he added a special 'couture' line to his growing ready-to-wear womenswear. His first shop, in Beauchamp Place, opened in 1984.

**Rifat Ozbek** Designer. Born 1954 in Istanbul, Turkey. Ozbek studied Architecture at Liverpool University and then took a degree in Fashion at St Martins School of Art. Following his graduation in 1977, he worked with the late Walter Albini at Trell in Milan, returning two years later to London, where he joined Monsoon as a designer. Ozbek formed his own company in 1984 and launched the 'O for Ozbek' T-shirt and denim line in 1987. He also produces a diffusion line called 'Future Ozbek'. He was named 'Designer of the Year' in 1988.

**Reynold Pearce** See **Pearce Fionda**

**Pearce Fionda** (Reynold Pearce and Andrew Fionda) Designers. Pearce (b. 1967, Middlesbrough, England) and Fionda (b. 1967, Leicester, England) met in 1985 at Nottingham Trent University, where they both studied Fashion. Pearce then worked in London for John Galliano before completing an MA at Central St Martins College of Art and Design in 1991. Fionda completed his MA at the Royal College of Art in 1990. After graduation, Pearce was appointed design assistant to Roland Klein while Fionda designed for companies in the UK and in Hong Kong. In 1994 they set up their own label, producing their first capsule collection in 1995. Pearce Fionda have won a number of awards for new designers. In 1997 they launched the Pearce II Fionda line for Debenhams.

**Fabio Piras** Designer. Born 1963 in Switzerland. Piras trained at Central St Martins College of Art and Design, graduating in 1993. His first collection was launched in Spring/Summer 1995.

**Mark Powell** Designer/bespoke tailor. Born 1960 in London, England. Powell is self-taught with a background in retail. In 1985 he opened his first shop, 'Powell and Co', based in the London's West End. Here he sold vintage clothes from the 40s, 50s and 60s and, as a sideline, provided a bespoke, made-to-measure service. He gave up this shop to establish an 'easy listening' night club, 'Violets', as a protest against the rave scene, but turned his attentions back to the clothing industry when he opened a bespoke business in 1989 in D'Arblay Street, moving to Newburgh Street in 1996. He launched his first collection in 1998.

**Antony Price** Designer. Born 1945 in Yorkshire, England. Price studied Fashion Design at Bradford College of Art until 1965, when he transferred to the Royal College of Art to take an MA in Design. From 1968 to 1976 he worked at Stirling Cooper and Plaza Clothing Company, designing mass-market retail clothing popularized by rock groups like the Rolling Stones and The Who. In 1976 he began to design record sleeves for various bands. In 1980 he presented his first ready-to-wear collection and opened a shop in South Molton Street in 1983. In 1990 he was named 'British Fashion and Glamour Designer of the Year'.

**Dai Rees** Milliner and accessories designer. Born 1961 in Bridgend, South Wales. Rees graduated from Central St Martins College of Art and Design in 1992 with a degree in Ceramic Design. He then completed an MA in Ceramics and Glass at the Royal College of Art, graduating in 1994. In 1996 he launched his own company, designing millinery and accessories. Rees has worked with a number of cutting-edge designers, including Julien MacDonald, Sonja Nuttall and Alexander McQueen.

**Serena Rees** See **Agent Provocateur**

**Zandra Rhodes** Textile designer. Born 1940 in Chatham, Kent. Rhodes graduated from Medway College of Art in Rochester in 1961, continuing her studies at the Royal College of Art, School of Textile Design, until 1964. She then worked as a dressmaker, textile designer and freelance designer before setting up her own company in 1975. She launched her first ready-to-wear collection in 1984.

**Inacio Ribeiro** See **Clements Ribeiro**

**John Rocha** Designer. Born 1953 in Hong Kong. Rocha arrived in London in the 1970s to study fashion at Croydon College of Art, graduating in 1977. He showed his first collection for Spring/Summer 1978. Since 1979 Rocha has lived in Dublin, Ireland, except for two years in the late 1980s, which he spent in Milan, perfecting tailoring and cutting techniques. He was named 'British Designer of the Year' in 1993 and in 1995 opened a showroom in Temple Bar, Dublin. Spring/Summer 1997 saw the successful introduction of the John Rocha Jeans range for men and women.

**Vicki L. Sarge** See **Erickson Beamon**

**Tanya Sarne** See **Ghost**

**Seraph** (Sherald Lamden) Designer. Born 1964 in London, England. With no formal training, Lamden gained experience in the late 1980s and the 1990s by working with various designers, in particular the Ghost design team. She created her first collection for Spring/Summer 1997.

**Emma Sewell** See **Wallace Sewell**

**Martin Simcock** See **Georgina von Etzdorf**

**Paul Smith** Designer. Born 1946 in Nottingham, England. Smith began his career in fashion at the age of 18 as a gofer in a clothing warehouse. In 1970 he opened, in Nottingham, one of the first boutiques outside London to stock designer clothes. After attending evening courses, Smith began designing garments himself. In 1976 he became a consultant to an Italian shirt manufacturer and to the International Wool Secretariat. Later the same year he started the Paul Smith label. Smith opened his first London shop in Covent Garden in 1979. In 1991 he launched a line of childrenswear, followed by womenswear in 1993 and spectacles and accessories in 1994. The company has more than 160 shops in Japan, as well as outlets in New York, Paris, Singapore and Hong Kong.

**Tomasz Starzewski** Designer. Born 1962 in London, England. Starzewski studied Fashion at St Martins School of Art before setting up his first business in 1981, working from a small studio in Fulham, London. In 1990 he opened a boutique on the Old Brompton Road in South Kensington, and in 1992 designed his first daywear collection. His flagship store in Sloane Street opened in 1996 and houses his entire range, including ready-to-wear, evening wear, couture and bridal wear. In 1998 Starzewski launched his first couture collection in the United States.

**Vanja Strok** See **Gharani Strok**

**Lars Sture** Jewelry designer. Born 1961 in Nordfjord, Norway. In 1992 Sture completed an MA in Jewelry Design at the National College of Art in Oslo, Norway. He also trained in London, at Central St Martins College of Art and Design. He established his business in 1993, presenting his first collection in Spring/Summer 1995. He has collaborated with Fabio Piras, Owen Gaster, Sonja Nuttall and Joe Casely-Hayford, among others.

**Suture** (Tom Adams and Philip Delamore) Designers. Adams (b. 1961, Belfast, Northern Ireland) studied Fine Art at Loughborough University and Printing at the Royal Academy, graduating in 1982. He then spent many years designing stage clothes. Delamore (b. 1968, Welwyn Garden City, Hertfordshire, England) graduated in 1990 with a degree in Fashion and Printed Textiles from Cheltenham & Gloucester College of Higher Education. They started their label at the end of 1995, presenting their first collection in 1996.

**Philip Treacy** Milliner. Born 1967 in County Galway, Ireland. Treacy studied at the National College of Art and Design in Dublin in 1988, before transferring to the Royal College of Art, London. While still a student, he worked for a number of designers, including Rifat Ozbek and John Galliano. Treacy's first business was established in Elizabeth Street,

London, and by 1991 he was working for Marc Bohan at Hartnell and for Victor Edelstein. He collaborated with Karl Lagerfeld in the summer of 1991 and continues to design for Chanel. In 1992 he created headdresses for a stage production of *My Fair Lady* and in 1993 produced a diffusion range for Debenhams, as well as presenting his first catwalk show.

**Georgina von Etzdorf** Textile designers. The company was founded in 1981 by three designers: Georgina von Etzdorf (b. 1955, Lima, Peru) and Martin Simcock (b. 1954, Widnes, Lancashire, England), both of whom studied Textile Design at Camberwell School of Art until 1977; and Jonathan Docherty (b. 1955, Stevenage, Hertfordshire, England), who trained in Industrial Design at St Martins School of Art, also graduating in 1977. Their first collection was shown in 1981.

**Amanda Wakeley** Designer. Born 1962 in Chester, England. Wakeley's company was founded in 1990, based initially in a small studio in London. Its Fulham Road flagship store opened in 1993. In 1996 Wakeley was awarded her third Glamour Award at the British Fashion Awards.

**Catherine Walker** Designer. Born in France. Walker moved to London after completing a doctorate in Philosophy at the University of Lille. She began her career in 1975, creating children's clothes, and in 1978 started the Chelsea Design Co. She founded her own label in 1991. She received the Designer of the Year Award for British Couture in 1991 and the Designer of the Year Award for Glamour in 1992. A number of her couture dresses for the Princess of Wales were included in the auction of the Princess's dress collection in 1997.

**Harriet Wallace-Jones** *See* **Wallace Sewell**

**Wallace Sewell** (Harriet Wallace-Jones and Emma Sewell) Textile designers. Wallace-Jones (b. 1965, Dorset, England) and Sewell (b. 1964, Norwich, England) studied Textile Design at Central St Martins College of Art and Design and Woven Textiles at the Royal College of Art, both graduating in 1990. In 1992 they began to produce their own scarf and throw collections.

**Tristan Webber** Designer. Born 1972 in Leigh-on-Sea, Essex, England. Webber studied part-time at Cordwainers College and completed an MA in Womenswear Design at Central St Martins College of Art and Design, graduating in 1997. He set up his label in the same year, launching his first collection in Spring/Summer 1997.

**Vivienne Westwood** Designer. Born 1941 in Glossop, Derbyshire, England. In partnership with Malcolm McLaren, Westwood began to design in 1970 at her shop at 430 King's Road. The shop metamorphosed from 'Let It Rock' in 1971 to 'Too Fast to Live, Too Young to Die' in 1972, 'Sex' in 1974, 'Seditionaries' in 1976 and 'World's End' in 1981. Westwood presented her first catwalk show – the Pirate collection – in 1981 and in 1982 began to show in Paris. Her collaboration with McLaren ended in 1983. Vivienne Westwood Ltd comprises three labels: Gold Label, Red Label and MAN. Westwood was awarded 'British Designer of the Year' in 1990 and 1991.

**Mark Whitaker** Designer. Born 1964 in Halifax, Yorkshire, England. Whitaker studied Fashion Design at Newcastle upon Tyne College of Art, graduating in 1986. Until 1995, when he began to design under his own label, he worked as Menswear Editor for the *Sunday Times Magazine* and as Fashion Editor for *British GQ* and *Details* (New York). He created his first collection for Autumn/Winter 1996–97.

**Matthew Williamson** Designer. Born 1971 in Chorlton, Manchester, England. Williamson trained in Fashion Design and Printed Textiles at Central St Martins College of Art and Design, graduating in 1994. He gained experience through placements in India and New York and also by working as an assistant to Zandra Rhodes. From 1996 he designed freelance for Marni, Georgina von Etzdorf and Monsoon, establishing his own company in the same year. He showed his first collection of womenswear for Spring/Summer 1997.

**Y.M.C.** (Frazer Moss and Jimmy Collins) Designers. Moss (b. 1966, Newport, Wales) had no formal design training, but worked during the 1980s for Vivienne Westwood before setting up the label Professor Head in 1991. Collins (b. 1966, London, England) worked for ten years at French Connection and started the label Komodo in the 1980s. The two designers formed Y.M.C, or You Must Create, in 1996 and presented their first collection for Autumn/Winter 1996–97.

## PUBLISHER'S ACKNOWLEDGMENTS

pp. 26–27 Styling Adam Howe. From 'Windows '97' story in *The Face*. pp. 30, 82, 83 Styling Jennifer Guerrini-Maraldi for *Country Life*. p. 47 Styling Karl Plewka. p. 51 Courtesy *Scene*. p. 79 Model Claudia Croft. pp. 84–91 Coordination and styling Claudia Croft. Thanks to Gideon Simeloff, Tony Collins, Tom Heaney, Shelly Thackral, Patrick Thomson, Michael Harvey and Todd. p. 104 Dusty 'O'. pp. 104, 141, 147, 183 Make-up artist Victor Alvarez Domenech. pp. 110, 121, 148 First published in *Dazed & Confused*. pp. 110, 121 Colour printing for Rankin by Chris Cooke, Metro Art. pp. 115, 149, 156, 157 Colour printing for Ram & Fab by Chris Cooke, Metro Art. p. 127 Rooftop access courtesy Sophy Cooper.

Thanks to Art Partner, Paris (p. 65), CLM Camilla Lowther Management, London (p. 117), Simon Costin (pp. 40– 41), East Photographic, London (pp. 26–27, 47), Izzy King, Art Dept. London (pp. 118–119), Aurélie Lambillon, Barry Lategan, Haidee Findlay Levin, M.A.P. Management and Production, London (p. 68), Andrea Rosenberg (pp. 168–169), and special thanks to Philip Stephens and Concrete PR, London.

## AUTHOR'S ACKNOWLEDGMENTS

The author wishes to thank the following:

Alexia Economou, Hazel Curry and Marc Karimzadeh, my brilliant researchers. Judge Jeffrey and the team at *Drapers Record* for their enormous support. Mum and Dad for financial support. All the PRs and designers for putting up with our incessant enquiries over the past year. And everyone who devoted their time and energy to making this project possible. Thank you.